# Life After This

## 9 Chapters: History Shows We Have Contacted the Deceased and You Can Do It, Too

**John Allen**

# Table of Content

This book is dedicated to three of the bravest angels who have left imprints in my heart. I wouldn't have had the inspiration to write this book if not for them. To Dad: *I know you're sitting on your heavenly perch watching over us.* To Mel: *I wish we'd had more time together but I know that you were needed elsewhere. I will take care of Alison for you.* And finally, to my little brother Amadeus: *Thank you for choosing me to be your human and trusting me to take care of you. I miss you more than words can say. Until I get there, take care of Dad and Mel.*

# Introduction

- Have you ever wondered what happens when someone you care about dies?

- Have you ever wondered if they are trying to reach out to you?

- Have you ever tried to reach out to them?

The death of a loved one is viewed as an inconvenience by those who are left behind. Oh, those who are left behind may even label the death of their loved ones as selfish. I mean, their audacity to leave this earth while we have so many unanswered questions is deplorable. We didn't have enough time to say and do everything we needed to. We didn't ask all the questions we needed answers to. We didn't get to say goodbye the way we wanted to.

The first leg of my journey to self-healing is detailed in my book *Keep Calm and Cope With Grief* where I introduced you to my personal story. I shared what I went through and experienced with the death of my father in November 2020. Writing that book helped me understand that grief has no rules and it can't be scheduled into your diary. Grief is a process everyone must go through at some point in their lives. Grief is not something that will wither away into the unknown. The grief you have experienced will always be embedded into your mind, body, and soul.

# Easing the Effects of Grief

This is an invitation for you to join me on the next leg of the journey to self-healing after experiencing grief. I know that many people will not agree with what is being discussed in this book, but I am not here to challenge anyone's beliefs or religion. I want to show you that many have embarked on similar journeys throughout the ages. Many have found these journeys to be helpful during the grieving process.

This book is going to focus on almost everything related to communicating with the dearly departed. No two people will experience the same grieving process and many will not agree with your decision to communicate with the dearly departed. Maybe your loved ones are trying to get your attention because all the signs they have left you have been ignored or not seen. I don't know what you have experienced, but I *do* know what I have seen. This journey of curiosity requires you to have an open mind, a lot of patience, and a dash of understanding.

The topics I will be covering during this journey include:

- an in-depth definition of life and death
- a stroll through the history archives to see how those before us communicated with the dearly departed
- a glimpse at various civilizations who have, and still do, practice their communication skills with the dearly departed
- an investigation into people's experiences regarding near-death experiences with some factual stories
- various methods to communicate with the dearly departed

- a look at what the Bible and other religions say about the afterlife

Have you been tickled by the curious elf? Dip your toes in the doubt pool and take a chance with me. What do you have to lose—a couple of hours while reading this book? I promise you that there will be no outlandish mind control techniques used to force you to do anything against your will. This book is going to help you during your grieving process. It is going to alert you to signs you may be missing. It may help you to close some doors and finally find closure.

## The Journey Begins Right Here

You may not believe that life after death exists. You may not believe that there is a spiritual connection that links us to our dearly departed. Not everyone's opinions will align with your beliefs. I am not going to be forcing my opinions and beliefs on you. I am still the same person I was when I wrote my last book. I am still held captive by the jaws of grief. I am a hostage because I feel the void that Dad left in my life. I am a hostage because I feel the emptiness that my trusted four-legged companion left in my life. Grief is not an option anyone chooses for pleasure.

I lost Dad to cancer in November 2020. It was the most difficult time of my life. I am still struggling, to this day, to come to terms with his passing. It is true that nobody gets over the loss of a loved one. Many people I have spoken with have shared that they feel the grief of their loved ones even when they didn't have good relationships with them. Seeing and hearing friends, loved ones, and strangers share their experiences prompted me to explore the idea of communicating with our dearly departed. I have many personal experiences that I will be sharing. Most of my experiences date back to before I knew about, or even considered, that communication with the afterlife was a real possibility.

My personal experience with grief has taught me that it is a never-ending loop. It is like the cycle on the washing machine or dishwasher that will keep on repeating. You are presented with 12 months, 52 weeks, and 365 days in a year. You will remember birthdays, anniversaries, Easter, Mother's/Father's Day, Thanksgiving, or Christmas Day. You may hear a favorite song, or walk into a room and smell a familiar scent. You are surrounded by constant reminders that don't have an on or off switch.

Grief neither ends nor vanishes into thin air, but it does change. Grief is a passage that allows you to travel through it. Grief is neither a sign of weakness, nor is it a lack of faith. Grief is the price you pay for the love you have for your dearly departed. Grief can hold you hostage because you are afraid to let go. Grief fills the most vulnerable part of your soul, which is both empty and sad. Grief is a foothold for thousands of questions that may be swimming through your mind.

I am, and have been, where you are. I am writing this book because I believe that grief led me here. Grief highlighted many of the questions I have stored in my mind. I am a curious person. I needed answers to help me understand what goes on around me. I have had many people tell me that I have a vivid imagination. Many have said that I have been making up stories for attention. I am almost certain that quite a few have wanted to have me committed to an asylum.

## *Seeing and Acknowledging Signs*

I believe that Dad has been trying to communicate with me since his passing. I have received many signs, which were too specific to ignore. I would find white feathers in places where you wouldn't expect to see them. I would hear the sound of a man's voice in my house—while I was alone. I know, without a shadow of a doubt, that Dad has been trying to reach out to me. It was this realization that led me to where I am now— writing a book about communicating with the dearly departed.

What would you do if you discovered that your dearly departed were leaving signs for you? Would you question these signs or would you find a way to interact with them? I have spoken to many people who have told me that they wouldn't know where to begin if they were to reach out to their loved ones. I had questions that I wanted answers to, but I had no one to ask for help and guidance. Those that I reached out to acted as if I were asking them to commit a sin. Others acted as if I was betraying my Catholic upbringing. I needed to know more; and, if I haven't already mentioned it before, I am curious. I want answers to questions. I have had many people ask me questions, and the questions I want answers to may help everyone else. I am hopeful that my questions will mirror those of people who are too afraid to use their voices. They may be anxiously waiting in the shadows for the answers they are longing for. Some questions include:

- How can I respond to my dearly departed?
- Is it possible to have a conversation with them?
- Can they hear us?

## Fact or Fiction: My 1999 Experience

The first story I am going to share with you may read like a script from an episode of *Ripley's Believe It or Not*. This is probably the first time I experienced someone or something trying to communicate with me from beyond the grave. Some may say that the following story is a work of fiction, but others may agree that it was a true experience. If you were to ask my daughter, who was with me when it happened, she would tell you that it was 110% factual.

As you may recall, I am a Liverpudlian who emigrated to the United States in early 2000. I was living in a three-bedroom house that was built in 1880. This house was home to me and my then five-year-old daughter, Jessica. I had joint custody of my daughter, who stayed with me from Monday to Friday and spent the weekends with her mum.

One Wednesday evening, I got Jessica ready for bed. I tucked her into her bed and kissed her goodnight. All was quiet and calm as I made my way to bed around midnight. Almost five minutes after I turned the lights out in my bedroom, I heard Jessica call me from her bedroom: "Daddy, can I sleep in your bed tonight?" I knew that my daughter struggled to sleep, and without hesitation, I responded, "Yes, come on then." I'm not entirely sure if my words were even out of my mouth before Jessica had crossed the landing, walked into my bedroom, and jumped into my bed.

## *The Voice: Part One*

In my house, I close the curtains at night and sleep with the bedroom door wide open. As I was trying to get comfortable, I heard a man's voice say, "John!" The voice made the hairs on the back of my neck stand to attention. It wasn't a voice I had heard before, and the tone had me likening it to what the devil may sound like. It was loud, deep, evil, and it made the room shake!

I bolted upright. Was my heart racing? No, it was trying to escape through my throat! I looked towards the bedroom door, where I believed the voice came from, but there was nothing but darkness. I was frozen as I listened for more sounds, but I heard nothing. Was I dreaming? Was I in one of those virtual reality games? What was going on? "What was that, Daddy?" Jessica asked beside me. Okay, so if I didn't say anything and Jessica asked, then we both heard the same thing. Well, I didn't want to scare my daughter, so I played it down and told her that it was a dog barking outside. I covered her up again and told her to go back to sleep. I lay back down and waited for my heart to settle. After staring at the entryway to my bedroom, I eventually drifted off to sleep.

The next day, Jessica and I were talking about this and that while walking to school. The conversation went to what had happened the previous night. I asked Jessica if she remembered hearing any strange noises. She looked up at me: "Yes Daddy, I heard someone call your name."

## The Voice: Part Two

All was well in the Allen household. I had convinced myself that the voice could possibly have been a sign of severe sleep deprivation. It had been two days since the 'voice' had been heard. Jessica was off to her mum's for the weekend, and I was planning on getting as much rest as I could. I didn't ever want to have a repeat of that scary event. Imagination or not, that voice—dripping with anger and hatred—was not a sound I wanted to hear, or imagine hearing, ever again.

I had the house to myself. What does a dad do when he is the king of the castle? He indulges in a glass of wine while soaking in the bath, with the soothing sounds of relaxing music surrounding him. Oh, I know that you realize where this story is going! I was sipping my wine when I heard the same voice: "John. John. John." The 'voice' said my name three times. This time around, it wasn't the same angry, evil, and loud voice that scared me two days previously. The voice called my name softly, which I would describe as a "come here" kind of call.

I was a lot calmer this time around, but yes, the hairs on the back of my neck did stand to attention again. However, my heart wasn't trying to escape from my chest. I calmly got out of the bath and, without spilling my wine, I pulled on my robe and started walking through all the rooms upstairs. I didn't see or hear anything. I made my way downstairs and continued my search, which yielded no results. All the entrances and windows leading in and out of the house were locked and secured.

I called my parents and when Mum answered, I told her that I had heard the voice again. Mum was adamant that she didn't want me staying there. She was more afraid than I was when I first heard the voice during the early hours of the morning. "John, get out of there! Come to our house!" I couldn't leave my house. I'm sure I made some promises to Mum before ending the call. I went to bed that night doing something I had never done before: I locked my bedroom door. It was a long shot, but it made me feel protected. Okay, I realize how this reads now; but, believe me, at the time it made sense to me.

### The Voice: Part Three

The following Tuesday evening, six days after the first encounter with the 'voice,' I was in the kitchen ironing some clothes. "John." I heard my voice friend call. This time my name was only called once. The 'voice' seemed to come from one of the upstairs rooms. I knew that I had a choice: I could let the fear of the voice grab me by the throat, or I could ignore it. I chose to ignore the voice and continue with my chores. It was the last time that I ever heard from my voice friend. Please stick around for the 'revelation' in Chapter 8.

## Let's Get This Show on the Road

People are quick to look at the cover of a book, read some pages from the beginning and end, and then dismiss it as being rubbish. The same can be said for documentaries or movies, where people will watch the first few minutes, skip to the end, and complain that the storyline made no sense. I would love to have you join me on this journey. I'm not going to insist that you believe everything I say, but I *am* going to ask you to trust me. Don't skim through everything just because you don't believe in the topic matter.

This topic is near and dear to my heart, and I have done a lot of research. The experiences I will share are true to me and the people who have reached out to me during my research. I am an advocate for the freedom of choice. I will not coerce anyone into changing their beliefs. All I ask is that you keep an open mind and form your own conclusions based on what *you* believe—not what your parents, siblings, church, or influencers believe. Listen to what is in your heart and mind. I am going to leave you with your thoughts as you continue on this journey.

I am going to share my beliefs with you, as well as what I perceive to be the truth. If we were to meet in the mall or at a coffee shop and you asked me: "Can I communicate with the dearly departed?" my answer would be a hard *YES!* I have shared my visions. I am re-issuing the invitation to join me on this journey of discovery. I am giving you permission to laugh, cry, swear, shout, or anything you need to get rid of pent-up frustrations. I would like this book to scratch those itches that have been left by the curiosity bug.

Come on, pop grief into your backpack. Throw in some tissues and whatever other comforts you may need. Fling your backpack over your shoulder and let's get this show on the road.

# Chapter 1:

# Understanding Life and Death—Exploring Various Interpretations

Every story has a beginning, a body, and a conclusion. Everything that you can see, smell, taste, or feel starts and ends somewhere. Am I overthinking things? I don't believe that I am, but many may disagree. I have previously shared that I am a very curious person. I need to investigate why an appliance in my home stops working. I need to figure out why the weeds in my garden flourish when they aren't being taken care of. Thanks to recent events in my life, I am determined to understand the science surrounding life and death.

I spoke to someone while doing research for my books, and they told me something that tickled my curious bug. They said that their mother loved to reminisce and share stories that had sentimental meaning to the relationship with their father. The stories would often start with: "When you were a twinkle in your father's eye..." They said that they had never fully understood what the idiom meant until later in life when they had a lightbulb moment. They realized that the stories being shared were from before their parents planned on having children. Hearing this made me think about the subject I want to explore for this chapter.

This book is not about "he said, she said" or "they're wrong, and you're right." Many people believe that death is the absolute end of someone's life. That is their perspective, and most likely their way of coping with their feelings. Many will not entertain the idea that their loved ones may be angels. That is their choice, and I am not going to try to change their views. I know what I choose to believe.

I believe in life after death. I believe that we can communicate with our dearly departed. I believe a lot of things that others may not agree with. I know that the world is not made up of my beliefs. It is your choice if you want to believe that the sun is yellow. It is your choice if you want to believe that the sky consists of 150 shades of blue, white, and gray. I want to find proof so that I can share my findings with others. Whatever proof I find may just be instrumental in helping others experience peace of mind and healing.

# The Beginning: The Facts of Life

I am not here to share my views on the meaning of life. Maybe one day, in the distant future, it would be an interesting subject to write about. Right now, however, I am here to uncover the facts that surround the question of life. Everyone knows what life is, but for the purpose of this book, let's take a look at a couple of statements:

- Life is when you breathe air into your lungs.
- Life is when you have a beating heart.

- Life is when you have blood coursing through your veins

- Life is when you feel emotions.

I am not going to dispute any of these statements because they are all correct. Everyone has a definition of what life means to them. I'm a member of the generation that didn't have computers, the internet, or access to search engines to look up important information. The closest I got to search engines and the internet was either a trip to the library, or relying on my parents, caregivers, or educators for information. However, this is not the definition of life I was searching for. I wanted more. I wanted to dig deeper. I wanted something that would help me prove a point.

## *Life: Dictionary*

I turned to the Merriam-Webster online dictionary. One definition indicates that life is an important element by showing the differences between a living person and a dead body. I do believe that the element being referred to is that a living person breathes, talks, and eats, as opposed to the non-responsive form of a person who has passed on. Another description defines life as being the period between the day you enter this world, and the day you leave this physical world (Merriam-Webster, n.d.-d).

# *Life: Science-Backed*

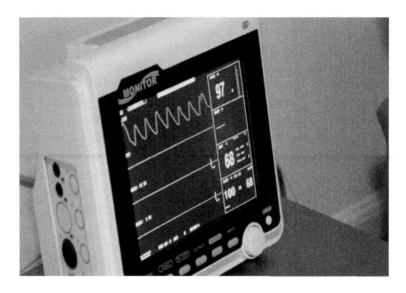

The layman's version may have been sufficient to satisfy the curious mind. However, the layman's definitions will not be enough to convince those whose beliefs are set in stone. The quest for science-backed definitions continues. I let my fingers do the clicking and my eyes do the reading, until I landed on Britannica's website.

The Encyclopedia Britannica's definition of life is consistent with what has been shared in the previous section. It tells us that the definition of life can be compared to, or is, living matter. What do we know about living matter? Anything that grows, reproduces, responds to stimulation, or adapts to its surroundings is living matter. Every single person walking around on this earth is made up of cells. These cells, also referred to as living matter, can take on the form of a person, an animal, or plant life that goes through the cycle of life (Sagan et al., 2018).

A visit to another online publication, the Khan Academy, gave me a little of a biology definition that I needed to incorporate into my findings. The article mentions that human beings are made up of multicellular organisms. The article explains that multicellular organisms have been arranged in such a way as to perform different functions in the body. This arrangement sees the cells separated and placed into various categories. The cells are fused to become tissues that help our bodies to function. The tissues in our bodies include the muscles and the nerves, and include the connective tissues. The various tissues in bodies are knitted together to form organs such as our hearts, lungs, kidneys, and liver. Each of the organs in our bodies has specific tasks. These tasks vary from person to person, but at the end of the day, the organs in our bodies act as a transport vessel that carries or distributes the necessary organisms that are vital to our existence. We wouldn't exist if it were not for these multicellular organisms (Khan Academy, n.d.).

## *Life: From the Word of God*

I believe that the Bible is the definition of life. Many will argue that the Bible is not a credible source of information because it has been 'recycled' one too many times. I'm not oblivious that the Bible has its flaws, and that there are gaping holes that got lost in translation. I love talking to people and hearing their opinions. I believe that it is important to listen to what each person has to say. I don't dismiss people because their beliefs don't align with mine. I like to think of myself as a people's kind of person who is easily approachable and always open to good, healthy banter.

One of the first mentions of human life in the Bible can be found in Genesis 2:7: "Then the Lord God formed a man from the dust of the ground and breathed into his nostrils the breath of life, and the man became a living being." All Bible verses have been taken from the New International Version (NIV). I'm not going to argue with the Bible because the very first words of Genesis 1:1 begin with the words: "In the beginning God created the heavens and the earth." These words, to me, are an indication that the earth had no living matter at the time when God set out to create the earth. It took God six days to prepare the earth for inhabitants. He took a well-deserved rest on the seventh day. Another indication that leads me to believe that the newly created earth was free of living matter is described in Genesis 2:5–6: "Now no shrub had yet appeared on the earth and no plant had yet sprung up, for the Lord God had not sent rain on the earth and there was no one to work the ground but streams came up from the earth and watered the whole surface of the ground." God created man so that he would nurture the earth and take care of the Garden of Eden.

The Bible has definitions for everything ranging from love and hate to peace and war, and everything in between. People are quick to throw scriptures around to prove that they are right and I am wrong. I believe that people are quick to want to prove you wrong when they are in a sinking boat. I have spoken to many people during the time when the global pandemic held us captive. It was thanks to the wonders of modern technology that we could interact via Skype, Zoom, or whatever video conferencing platform was available. The Christian population is made up of people who take everything in the Bible literally, those who dig deeper and form their own interpretations (open-minded individuals), or those who have memorized the important bits of the Bible to throw around without understanding the meaning behind it.

I have previously shared that I am open-minded. I am not ashamed of my beliefs. I am not afraid to be curious. God loves me with all my warts, my extra toe, and every imperfect part of me because, in His eyes, I am perfect. What else does the Bible say about life? Romans 4:17 says: "As it is written: "I have made you a father of many nations." He is our father in the sight of God, in whom he believed—the God who gives life to the dead and calls into being things that were not." God gives us life. It is because of Him that we inhabit the earth and walk around freely. We are life, and it is because of each person that moves on this earth that the cycle of life will continue through the generations to come.

## The End: The Facts of Death

All living matter on this earth follows a cycle, which is known as the *cycle of life*. It may take a minute for some to understand the concept, but it is important to understand that everyone and everything follows a cycle. You cannot pause, resume, hit the fast-forward button, and expect to start over if you have messed up. The cycle of life starts the day you are born, and ends the day you let out your last breath.

Death is not something everyone likes to think about. Many may think that death is the enemy that breaks up families and destroys their worlds. Others may think that death is unnecessary and unfair—especially when it involves children. I think it is safe to assume that death is something that causes pain in the hearts and souls of people across the globe. I am going to transition to my alter ego, Professor John Allen, and don my lab coat for the next leg of this discovery journey. I am going to dig through the piles of dust to uncover what death means in the sphere of science.

- Where does the spirit or soul go after death?

- Is the spirit or soul a form of gas that evaporates upon death?

- What happens to the physical body when someone dies?

I must admit that I have had some time to think about the questions that I would like to be answered during this journey of discovery to the afterlife. The questions I have must have been buried in my subconscious, because they suddenly appeared in my thoughts shortly after Dad passed on. Come on, let's continue on this quest to look at some of the definitions I have found of what death may mean.

## *Death: Dictionary*

Many may say that they don't need a definition to understand what death is. Others may be shuffling their feet uncomfortably because they have their opinions. Remember, not everyone shares the same views. I am not searching for definitions to make people feel uncomfortable about what they believe or do not believe. I need to do this because I am out to prove to myself that there is a life after this. One of the first definitions that the Merriam-Webster online dictionary shares is that death occurs when all the vital organs of the body cease to function. Another entry suggests that death is the loss of life, or the state of not being part of the human race. None of the definitions can be disputed because, at the end of the day, they are all correct (Merriam-Webster, n.d.-b).

## *Death: Science-Backed*

I stumbled across many different types of resources that would attempt to give me definitions of what they perceive to be the science behind death. One such resource was an article written for the Deutsche Welle, a German international broadcasting agency that prides itself on reporting relevant and factual information. The article, which is titled *The Science of Dying*, is written by Alexander Freund.

Freund's article defines death as the process of one's body having aged, and it reaching the end of its cycle. Aging is a natural progression that everyone goes through and, while many don't want to acknowledge that they are getting on in years, it has to happen. No amount of self-care, nips, tucks, or vitamins are going to help your organs as they go through the necessary aging process. I don't think anyone is going to argue or dispute that a great amount of care has gone into making sure that you live a long, happy, and healthy life. The organs in your body do age and, unfortunately, (as far as the aging process goes) the organs will stop working. Someone told me that life means that *eventually everything stops working*. This is the cycle of life.

Freund explains that a clinical death occurs when the organs that keep the heart beating, and lungs breathing, stop working. The body is being deprived of the necessary nutrients and oxygen that keep everything working like a well-oiled machine. What about shocking someone or performing CPR on someone that is clinically dead? Freund tells us that someone who has clinically died could be resuscitated. My interpretation of this scenario would be if someone's heart stopped and they were brought back to life by way of being shocked in the hospital, or someone was to perform CPR until a medical professional arrived at the scene. Resuscitation is mostly performed on people who have been in an accident or suffered some kind of trauma. People who have been diagnosed with incurable illnesses, or have reached an age where they are ready to join their loved ones, may have signed medical waivers that prevent resuscitation.

A person who has been declared brain-dead may still have all their organs working, but they are being kept alive with machines. The machines are necessary because the brain can't tell the organs what to do anymore. I have seen and heard about instances where, when the patient is declared brain-dead, the family and loved ones are not ready to turn the machines off. They would rather hold onto hope that their loved ones will wake up from their unconscious state (Freund, 2019).

## *Death: From the Word of God*

I think that everyone would like to believe that they are immortal. I also know that many people go about their daily lives believing that they will defy death. If only it were that easy. I believe that people are afraid of the unknown. The thought of not having control over your life when you reach the end of the life cycle is scary. I am aware that people are afraid of death because they do not know what will happen when they die.

Everyone is quick to dismiss the scriptures because they don't believe that there is anything in there that is beneficial to their life or circumstances. I love the idea of referring to the Bible as a manual. It may not be your typical *IKEA* manual that gives you step-by-step instructions, but I do believe that the Bible is packed with information that is essential to your life and whatever you may be going through. I know that the Bible was written before Christ was born. I also know that it may even have been translated more than a thousand times. I deem, which may be an unpopular belief, that history is being repeated. I only have to turn on the television, open a newspaper, or listen to the radio to hear what is going on out there in the world. I was around when a global pandemic was declared, and the world stepped on its brakes to slow down. What about the riots, people fighting, murder, wars, famine, and even the changes in the weather patterns? The Bible is showing us what has, is, and will happen.

The Bible tells us about two types of deaths. One is physical, and the other is spiritual. It is important to look at both definitions. I believe that it may be what I am looking for to show naysayers that the afterlife may be real. The first definition of death that I found came as no surprise to me. You may recall the Bible's definition of life, and the verse from Genesis 2:7 where it is said that "God formed a man from the dust of the ground and breathed into his nostrils the breath of life…" I would like to turn your attention to Ecclesiastes 12:7: "… and the dust returns to the ground it came from, and the spirit returns to God who gave it." The definition of physical death clearly indicates that the spirit becomes separated from the body. It is evident that the body is a placeholder, or vessel, in this physical world. Our bodies are on loan for the duration of our stay in the physical world. Our spirits live in these temporary vessels until our destiny on this earth has been fulfilled. The body will return to the ground. Where does our spirit go once God calls it home?

I have heard people say that God has forsaken them because of everything that is going wrong in their lives. Others have said that *God doesn't care, because if He did, why are people dying of cancer,* or *why is He allowing people to go hungry?* You may not believe me, and you may not believe what the scripture tells you, but I can tell you that God will never forsake you, me, or any person that lives on this planet. God loved you when He knit you together in your mother's womb, and He will love you until the day you return to Him. God doesn't give life only to take it back as a punishment.

A spiritual death is when humans separate themselves from God. The Bible tells us in 1 Corinthians 15:21–22: "For since death came through a man, the resurrection of the dead comes also through a man. For as in Adam all die, so in Christ all will be made alive." Ephesians 4:18 shares: "They are darkened in their understanding and separated from the life of God because of the ignorance that is in them due to the hardening of their hearts."

I strongly believe that every day that I am alive is a gift that God has given me. Life is a gift. Death is a gift. What happens to our spirits when our bodies expire? That is why I am here. I am going to travel the road that many are afraid to wander down. You may hide behind me. I will guide you as best I can. Always remember that God will always love you because, in His eyes, you are His most treasured possession. I will not force you to continue if you don't feel comfortable. Take a deep breath in through your nose, and exhale slowly through your mouth. I'll see you in the next chapter.

# Chapter 2:

# Stepping Out of Your Body—

# Experiencing Life Without a

# Filter

The title of this chapter is an indication of the direction in which the next leg of this journey is heading. I pride myself on being someone who is mindful and takes everyone's feelings and state of mind into account. I know what it is like to enter a situation and not know which way to turn. This is where grief seems to linger. I spoke about the "cloak of grief" in my previous book. I also mentioned that the cloak has many layers, and it is up to each person who is on that journey to work through the layers at a comfortable pace.

Grief is also a trickster that has you believing in something you wish were true. On the one hand, your mind is telling you that whatever it is you are thinking about is a fabrication, or a manifestation, of what you are hoping for. On the other hand, your heart is telling you to go with whatever you need to help ease the pain you are experiencing. You know, and I know, that grief is not something that goes away because someone tells you that you need "to get over it" or to "stop looking for attention." No one will ever understand what someone is going through until they are sitting in the same rocking chair.

The need to see, feel, or chat with your loved ones is part of the grieving process. I had someone tell me that they would give anything to have five minutes with their dearly departed loved one. They were asked why they would need those five minutes if they had a lifetime. They were then told, in no uncertain terms, to leave the dead alone. I saw the anguish in this person's eyes as they shared this experience with me. They asked me if they were being selfish by wanting that five-minute visitation—my response was no, because I want that, too. I asked them if they believed that their loved ones were still around—their response, without hesitation, was *YES*.

Part of my research found me watching and listening to many TEDx Talks on YouTube and podcasts, as well as reading articles about near-death experiences (NDE). Some may say that I am obsessed with the topic, and others may want to have me committed to the asylum. I cannot help that I have an insatiable curiosity that draws me to want to have just one more visit with Dad, or an hour to rough-and-tumble with Amadeus (my dog). This journey that I have embarked on is taking me through many twists and turns. I know, and acknowledge, that this is not an easy journey. I also believe that the difficulty of this journey is helping me, and others, work through the layers of grief.

# The Unfiltered Experience: Near-Death Experiences

This journey, or need, to understand if there is an afterlife and what it is about has had me thinking about some questions. One such question I have been wondering about is whether there is a prelude to death. You know, something similar to a preview or a glimpse as to what is waiting for the broken and diseased body when it leaves one world for another. The people who want to have me committed to the asylum are laughing at me because I am 'contradicting' what I have said in the previous chapter. I know that the definition of death, as described by the Bible, is that the body and spirit become separated. I have also previously mentioned that the Bible is open to interpretation. Yes, the physical body is returned to dust. I am not going to dispute that. I also know that the soul or spirit of someone is returned to God. I would like to believe that the soul or spirits of our loved ones are given celestial bodies that allow them to flit around from one place to the next. I also like to believe that celestial beings are angels. However, talks about celestial beings are a discussion for another chapter.

I believe that this chapter is going to be the one that will awaken some memories you have hidden within the crusty and dusty archives in your mind. This chapter is strategically placed to keep you thinking about the details as you continue with your discovery journey. Some people may be sitting upright, finger on this page, and saying: "A-ha!" You know, those people who are trying to disprove everything that I believe in. They may be thinking, and convincing themselves, that this is my attempt at controlling the minds of my readers. I'll share a little secret with everyone—this is not, and will never be, some type of mind-controlling tactic. Doubter friends, relax. This is my journey that I have invited you, and everyone else, to be part of. I have told you before that I believe that everyone has the freedom of choice to do whatever they want. Everyone has their reasons for joining me on this journey. I also believe that the one thing that brought everyone here is *grief.* Together, we are going to learn how to cope with the aftermath of a loved one's passing.

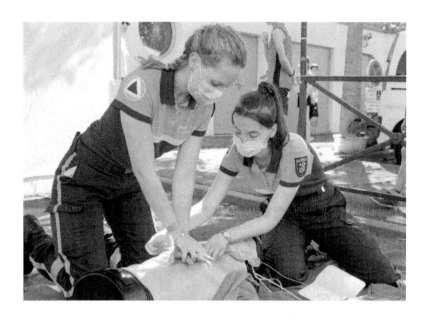

## Definition of a Near-Death Experience

Could the near-death experience be a prelude to what is waiting
on the other side? Let's see what the Merriam-Webster online
dictionary has to say. A near-death experience is described as
someone who has stared death in the eye after experiencing a
traumatic event. I have heard many people say that they have
"seen their lives flash before their eyes," and I can only imagine
that this is the experience they may have encountered. The
definition continues with a theory that the traumatic event
could be linked to a spiritual experience. The person having the
experience may see their loved ones who have passed away, see
a playback of their own lives, or possibly even be a witness to a
bright, white light that is inviting them to enter another world
(Merriam Webster, n.d.-e).

- Is it so difficult for people to have an open mind?

- What is wrong with allowing the grief-stricken family members to cling to hope that their loved ones are still with them?

- What gives anyone the right to decide what someone else should or should not be feeling?

It is no secret that I am fascinated by the topic of near-death experiences, the afterlife, and everything remotely related to proving that there is a life after this. Medical professionals, ranging from psychiatrists and neurologists to emergency trauma doctors and nurses, have shared their findings in articles, medical journals, and TEDx Talks. I am truly baffled when people I interact with—whether friends, loved ones, acquaintances, or strangers—are skeptical or look at me as if I've lost all my marbles. Why is it easier for people to skip over the science, facts, or figures, and go straight to the conspiracy theories, social media posts, or hate-spewing tabloids?

If you haven't already, I would like to encourage you to read my previous book, *Keep Calm and Cope With Grief: 9 Chapters for Managing Fear and Grief When Losing a Parent or Loved One*. This book will give you a detailed explanation of how people experience the loss of a loved one in different ways. I have previously mentioned that some people may want to hold onto the idea that their dearly departed are still guiding them, or believe that their loved ones are making sure that they are okay.

## A Closer Look at Near-Death Experiences

It is important to keep in mind that not everyone will have the same experiences. Each experience may sound like one you have heard before, but listening to the details will alert you that it is different. It does get under my skin when someone starts sharing their recollection of events as it happened to them, and someone comes in and says: "Oh yes, that happened to me, too." I have often praised myself for keeping my mouth zipped, and I am pretty sure that Dad may also be covering my mouth so that I don't say anything. I love listening to stories and, yes, some may seem repetitive; but, when I hear the same story from someone who doesn't know the other person, or who lives in another state or country, I take notes—lots of them. Another one of my unpopular beliefs is that everyone has had a near-death experience at some point in their lives.

I am pretty sure that I recently had a near-death experience while training for a cycling event. It is no secret that motor vehicles don't have much patience when it comes to sharing the road with cyclists. I was well within my bike lane when a car decided that it needed more space. That need for more space brought up visions of my life, from birth to adulthood, that flashed before my eyes. I don't know much of what happened, but I do know that I was not ready to cross over into the bright light that was beckoning me. I managed to gain control of my bicycle, stop, and calm down as the car sped off. You may be saying that I'm a coward for not "being ready to cross over" but there is a little bit of method behind my madness. The most important reason, I believe, is that I know my destiny has not yet been fulfilled. How do I know that my destiny has not been fulfilled? Call it intuition if you want, but I do believe that God isn't ready for me to go home just yet. He did, however, give me a play-by-play of my life—which could mean that I have some people I need to reach out to, or I need to be the pillar of strength for my family back in Liverpool or my fiancé and Jessica here in the United States. Who knows, maybe I am writing this book to answer the question about why I didn't succumb to the near-accident.

## Studies Relating to Near-Death Experiences

I wanted to present you with some facts based on studies conducted by medical professionals. The information shared in this section is not hearsay or an "I heard it from my aunt, who heard it from her hairdresser, who heard it from her neighbor, who heard it from the farmer two counties away" scenario. I have a moral obligation to be truthful, or I will receive a cuff on the ear from Dad where he is watching me from his heavenly perch.

# The Seven Categories Relating to Near-Death Experiences

Fiona MacDonald wrote an article for the Science Alert online publication based on a study conducted at the Stony Brook University School of Medicine. The study, orchestrated by the director of resuscitation research at the University, Sam Parnia, has interviewed over 100 patients who have reportedly had near-death experiences. These patients were resuscitated after suffering cardiac arrests. Parnia's extensive interviews and research concluded that the near-death experiences could be categorized into seven different groups. Let's take a look at each of the categories, and see what they tell us. Everything we learn is one step closer to the journey of discovering what is waiting for us after this life (Parnia et al., 2014, pp. 1799–1805).

### Fear

Many people fear death. No one knows why that fear exists. Is it the fear of pain? Is it the fear of not knowing what is going to happen? Is it the fear that you will be walking into a trial where you will be judged for your past? If you read the Bible, John

3:16 tells us: "For God so loved the world that he gave his one and only Son, that whoever believes in him shall not perish but have eternal life."

## *Bright Light*

A psychiatrist by the name of Bruce Greyson spent years doing research based on the near-death experiences shared by his patients. Greyson has written many books on his findings. In an article written for the *Guardian Weekly*, Alex Moshakis shares Greyson's story in an article titled: "What Do Near-Death Experiences Mean, and Why Do They Fascinate Us?" Greyson shares a patient's recollection of their experience where they say that they were standing in a meadow, completely clear-minded, lucid, and knowing who they were. They remembered that the meadow was surrounded by a radiant light. They say that they had never seen a light so vibrant and beautiful in the real world. The encounter continued with a description of the plants that were growing in the meadow. The patient said that each of the plants in the meadow was omitting a gentle, and soft, flicker of light which made the scene around them even more radiant (Moshakis, 2021).

## *Animals*

This section is based entirely on research done by me. The studies relating to having an experience with animals or nature are few and far between. I came across information, written by Scott Janssen for the online publication, *The Bark*, and titled: "Near Death Experiences: Will Our Dogs be Waiting For us?" In the article, Janssen interviews Janice Holden, EdD, LPC-S, LMFT who is the editor of the *Journal of Near Death Studies*. Janssen writes that even though many people have shared that their near-death experiences allowed them to see their dearly departed pets, Ms. Holden is adamant that there has been no systematic study done that could deny or confirm these heartwarming stories.

I have previously mentioned that I am not here to choose sides. I maintain that if the person who had the near-death experience saw their beloved pets, then that is who they saw. I recently met up with a friend for coffee and a chat. I told them that I could feel my dog's presence. Where I would have asked questions to find out more, the friend dismissed me, basically telling me that animals don't go to heaven. Well, I am sorry, but I will believe what I have always believed, and know that one day I will be reunited with Dad, Amadeus, and all the pets I've had over the years.

## Déjà Vu

Do you recall me mentioning that just about everyone has possibly had a near-death experience during their lifetime? Déjà vu is recognized as one of the seven categories of near-death experiences that people have recalled during the research and study process. The Merriam-Webster online dictionary defines déjà vu as being in a setting and reliving a sequence of events as if it had already occurred. Another definition would be when your senses are triggered into remembering that you may have seen, heard, and experienced something before it had happened (Merriam-Webster, n.d.-c).

I had always believed that near-death experiences involved visions of people who were going to die, and it never occurred to me that they could also be visions. I spoke to someone who shared their déjà vu experience with me. The lady shared that she had dreamed that her father, who had terminal cancer, was going to die that day. Her mother told her, in her dream, that her father was not doing good. She jumped out of bed and ran down to the master bedroom. When she entered the room, she saw her grandparents sitting on either side of her father, who had a smile on his face. The lady was then pulled from her dream by her mother waking her up by saying that her father was not doing good. She jumped out of her bed and ran to the master bedroom to find her father laying there. She looked for her grandparents, only to realize that they had come to tell her that they would be taking him. This lady had never told anyone of this dream until many years later. Many of her family thought she was making up stories, but a look at her mother's face let her know that she did believe her.

Déjà vu is not limited to seeing or predicting the death of someone, but it is also about experiencing the sense of already having done something. Whether it was in a previous life, or a premonition of what was to come, is uncertain. This is my reasoning when I say that everyone has had near-death experiences without realizing it. They may not have known what it was called, or understood what it was about, but it certainly has happened.

### Violence and Persecution

Michael N. Marsh wrote an article for the Wolfson College at the University of Oxford in the United Kingdom titled: *"The Near-Death Experience: A Reality Check?"* The article looks at near-death experiences as collected during various interviews with people who were willing participants to share their stories. The research and study indicate that not too many people are willing to talk about their nightmarish near-death experiences. Marsh mentions that statistics have indicated that more than 700,000 people have experienced a version of 'hell' that may be too upsetting to recollect. People may not want to share their near-death experiences because talking about them could open up a can of worms that don't need to be unleashed. These experiences could be traumatic, too violent, very vivid, and/or terrifying.

Marsh continues to say that the individuals who had shared their recollections had experienced intense darkness, a sense of all the air being sucked out of the space they were in, or falling without landing on any solid ground. They recalled hearing sounds that could be described as screams, or unearthly noises. Others have said that they saw creatures that they had never seen before and experienced feelings of panic, anxiety, fear, and being alone with nobody to reach out to for support (Marsh, 2016, p.18).

## *The Welcoming Committee: Family Reunion*

I believe that the most common near-death experience is finding yourself face-to-face with your dearly departed loved ones. Seeing your family doesn't mean that it is your time to join them. I also believe that the dearly departed are waiting to give us messages from God to tell us that our job on earth has not yet been fulfilled. I can feel the naysayers shaking their heads because "not everyone had a happy family" life. I believe, very strongly, that family does not have to be from your bloodline. Family is anyone, from friends to people who treat you like one of their family. You don't have to share DNA to be considered part of a family.

I recall a story I heard from someone about a 96-year-old lady that had defied death more times than could be counted on two hands. Her granddaughter went to visit her as often as she could. The grandmother had dementia, but she remembered everything before 2018, in detail. One day, when the granddaughter went to visit, her grandmother asked her when she was going to die. She was tired and wanted to go home. The granddaughter joked with her and told her that they weren't ready for her up in heaven. She reminded her of the time she had a stroke and told her that her grandfather had probably guffawed her and sent her back, saying she had not finished what she had started on earth. They laughed and her grandmother accepted the answer—until it was repeated the next time she went to visit. After three years of side-stepping death—having had a stroke, broken her hip, had double pneumonia, and fallen more times than anyone would like to admit—her grandmother passed away with a smile on her face. The granddaughter believed, without a doubt, that she was greeted by her husband, her daughter, her son-in-law, and all her family who had all passed away many years before.

## *Out of Body Experience*

The last category of our discovery of near-death experiences directs us to an article written by Jeffery Long, MD, titled: *"Near-Death Experiences Evidence for Their Reality."* Near-death experiences are not limited to a person's location. These experiences are not targeting a specific type of person based on their age, gender, ethnicity, standing in the community, or their beliefs or non-beliefs. Long states that 17% of people, from all walks of life and geographical locations, are reported to have experienced a near-death experience. I also find it ironic that he says what I have been saying since I started this book—that no two people will have the same near-death experience (Long, 2014, p. 132).

In the same article, Long shares something by the psychiatrist, Bruce Greyson, as mentioned in this chapter under the heading of "Bright Light". Greyson states that approximately 22% of near-death experiences happened when patients were put under general anesthetic. These patients have recalled saying that they had watched doctors or medical professionals performing procedures. They also recalled seeing bright lights, seeing family members who had passed on, or experiencing thoughts and memories that presented to them as clear as day (Holden et al., 2009).

Other out-of-body experiences are believed to happen when the heart and lungs stop working, and before the brain suffocates with a lack of oxygen and no blood flow. During this time, medical professionals will perform resuscitation. Patients have, as mentioned in the previous paragraph, recalled that they had been separated from their bodies and were watching what was happening to their bodies.

# *Thinking Inside the Box: Author's Thoughts*

This chapter has been filled with science-based facts, research, and studies. Everything that has been cited is available for your reading pleasure, which can be found in the reference section at the end of this book. I know that many people will have a hard time with the subject matter that has been discussed in this chapter. It is not, and was not, my intention to create hurtful memories or to fill anyone with fear.

It is my belief, whether popular or unpopular, that everyone needs to know that they do not have to be afraid of the unknown. One only has to read the studies and research, or the stories that I have shared, to know that nobody has to be afraid to know what is on the other side. I believe that everyone has a right to be curious, and no one has the power to force their beliefs on others. It is not a sign of weakness to follow your instincts or gut feeling. I could share a million stories that relate to what is presently happening all across the globe. It is only natural that I am curious, spurred on by my grief, where I want to know more.

Join me in the next chapter, where I am going to try my best at interpreting what the Bible, and different religions, say about the time when we leave this physical earth. I would like to remind you that you are safe here. You will not find any condemnation or judgment hidden in the words or between the pages of this book. You may be here because you are looking for something. You may be here because you don't understand how to interpret the flame that is burning in your soul. You may even be here because you are still looking for ways in which to deal with your grief. Come on, let's slide on over to the next chapter.

Chapter 3:

# The Christian Life—Exploring

# the Afterlife

Would you believe me if I told you that God is 10 steps ahead of you at all times? He knows what you are going to do before you have even thought about it. God knows that we will stray. He knows that we will do things that will make many people frown. We're human, and we're allowed to explore. I have known people who have smoked, drank, and done things that would make anyone question why they are still alive. The short answer to that question is that God never gave up on them. Their destiny had not yet been fulfilled. He also knew that, at the end of the day, everyone will find their way back to His loving arms.

## Religion: Through My Eyes

As you know by now, I was raised in the Catholic Church. I was an altar boy at my local church and school. I also attended all-boys Catholic schools in Liverpool. At one stage, during my teenage years, I was convinced that I wanted to be a priest. As you may have gathered, I didn't become a priest; but, I never gave up on my religion and faith. In fact, I am still in contact with Father Pat, the priest from the Catholic church in my hometown, Liverpool. Father Pat is always willing to listen and offer valuable resources without making me feel like a failure.

I attended church every Sunday. I sang the hymns along with the congregation. I diligently lit candles and prayed for everyone that needed prayers. In short, I was doing everything that I was taught to do by my parents, the schools, and the church. It is our parents' and educators' 'jobs' to shape our minds while we are in our formative years. Our childhoods consist of a base structure that is initiated in the home. Our parents teach us everything they know, and they will continue with their teachings until we are old enough to make decisions for ourselves.

I have always had an open and curious mind while growing up. I believe that the older I get, the more curious I am becoming. I do believe in science and facts. My beliefs and curiosity are not a reflection of where I am in my faith. It wasn't until Dad was diagnosed with cancer that I started asking questions. It was as though a boarded-up room in an old, rickety home had been pried open, and all the questions came tumbling out. These questions, paired with my grief, have prompted me to set out on this journey and to take as many willing (or non-willing) companions along for the ride. The only requirements for this journey are that you have an open mind. This is still your safe space where you cannot, and will not, be judged for your curiosity.

- Have you ever wondered who can hear your prayers?

- Where do your prayer requests end up?

- Have you ever wondered who can hear your conversations with God?

- What about the hymns you sing?

- Who are you singing to?

- Is singing one of those communication channels where you can communicate with God or loved ones?

- What happens with those silent prayers that don't pass your lips?

## A Glimpse at Christianity

I had never thought about challenging any of the practices I diligently participated in while growing up. I didn't think about turning to the history archives to see my burning questions and answers. I had been a sponge who soaked up everything. I never had any reason to ask questions. It had never occurred to me that there was a whole world beyond the scope of what I was taught. I have often heard people ask why someone would want to fix something that isn't broken. I may have been the one uttering those sentiments after Dad's passing. Grief opened up some doors that I never knew existed. The burning questions were screaming for answers.

I am, and have always been, strong in my faith. This didn't mean that I wasn't allowed to be curious. The curious part of my brain wanted to know more. I found myself here because I wanted answers. I wanted all the facts I would lay my hands on. I wanted to understand what role the facts played in my life. I needed to figure out what the driving force behind my faith was. I started watching many documentaries about Christ, the Holy Grail, the crucifixion, and different religions and denominations. I was fascinated when researchers and scientists found evidence or scriptures that showed that the Bible wasn't just stories that were made up. Historians have validated the scriptures and stories in the Bible as being authentic. There were also those who made it their mission in life to prove that the scriptures and stories in the Bible were fabricated.

# Religion: Through the Eyes of Religious Denominations

I think it is very safe to assume that each denomination in the religious sphere has its own beliefs about what happens when we die. I have also previously mentioned that we have many believers who follow the scripture word for word. They will not even begin to entertain the idea of challenging the word of God. I have met many people who believe that the Bible should be followed literally, and that there is no way that anything is open to interpretation. I will admit that I do get a little bothered by these types of people. I also believe that, if we were following and practicing the Bible literally, the second coming would have occurred and we would have been swept up in the rapture.

I have found that you cannot argue or make someone see things through your glasses because every vision is different. I believe that we are conditioned, from a tender age, to learn everything like a parrot. Sunday school lessons more often than not teach children Bible verses that they are expected to remember. I recently saw a reel on Instagram where an influencer was teaching his three-year-old daughter to recite Bible verses. You may be thinking that there is nothing wrong with that. I wouldn't have a problem with it, either, but I do feel that this is something everyone has gone through in their lives. They are made to remember verses, and when it is time for them to branch out and find their own path in life, they are afraid to explore or be curious because of the way they have been taught.

## *A Closer Look at Religious Denominations, Beliefs, and Practices*

I hemmed and hawed about how to start this section, and decided that whichever direction I veered towards, God would guide me to where I needed to be. One of the first things I feel I need to do is give you a definition of what the soul and spirit are. A glance at my trusted Merriam-Webster online dictionary tells me that, even though they may have similar meanings, they are different.

The soul is defined as being the part of who a person is. Every person has a soul, that one may call a flame of life. It is an important part of every human being. It is also believed that the soul acts as a moral compass, and helps people tap into their emotional sides. I think it is safe to assume that if someone doesn't have a soul, they would no longer be considered to be alive and walking amongst us (Merriam-Webster, n.d.-f).

The spirit is defined as being of a supernatural nature. It is most commonly a reference to the Holy Spirit which, as you know, is part of the Holy Trinity as described in the Bible, who are God the Father, Jesus Christ the Son, and the Holy Spirit. The word 'spirit' has various definitions, such as leading one to believe that the spirit is important to giving life to physical organisms. Another definition would be that of possibly being a harmful entity that will enter and possess a person that is vulnerable and possibly doubting their position in their life's journey (Merriam-Webster, n.d.-g).

These two definitions are important when it comes to adding to the knowledge we have about life and death. Chapters 1 and 2 have been instrumental in getting us to this part of the chapter where we look at the different religious practices and beliefs of the various denominations within the Christian faith. I was born and raised in the Catholic Church. I know people who are members of the Methodist Church, Baptist Church, and the Church of Latter-Day Saints. I have also heard about believers who belong to the Jehovah's Witness church, Hillsongs, and many others. I am not here to share my opinions about the different branches in denominations. Each person has to follow their heart. I am here to learn about what happens when we step out of this life we currently find ourselves in.

I have picked a couple of the denominations to see what they have to say about death, and the possibility of life *after* this death. The question we are going to have branded in our minds as we continue on this journey is: "Is there a life after this one?" I believe that I already have my answer, but please don't let my beliefs influence yours. We are adults, and we have the freedom to think for ourselves.

## Catholic Faith

I stumbled across a blog post on the Join Cake website that was written by Sarah Kessler and titled: "What Does the Catholic Church Teach About the Afterlife?" Kessler starts off her post by stating the Christian religious beliefs in the afterlife stem from the resurrection of Jesus. Kessler continues her article by highlighting God's original plan for humans to spend eternity at His side after dying. This plan is said to have been halted because of the transgression of disobedience by Adam and Eve in the Garden of Eden. Members of the Catholic faith believe that the pain and suffering of someone nearing the end of their life is part of the penance being paid for the disobedience of Adam and Eve.

Kessler's article covers all the bases of dying, death, and the funeral that follows. The big question we all want answered is: "Is there life after this one?" The answer would be hopeful. Kessler writes that members of the Catholic faith believe that they will see God. They also believe that they will be surrounded by saints and angels who are of Catholic descent. It is believed that heaven is where the souls will feel the love, joy, and happiness of God and celestial beings.

## The Church of Jesus Christ of Latter-Day Saints (LDS)

Members of the LDS Church, also commonly referred to as Mormons, believe that they will be reunited with the dearly departed in the afterlife. I have spoken to many people who don't agree with the LDS religion or their beliefs. I have seen a couple of wordy social media posts; but, as I have said before, I am not here to break down or speak out about other people's beliefs or religions. I still strongly believe that when we die, we will all end up standing before the same God, or whatever you may want to call Him. I am fascinated by the LDS religion because of all their beliefs, teachings, and views surrounding life and lifestyles. Again, I'm not going to say that I agree with everything, but it is interesting to explore.

Members of the LDS Church believe that our bodies and spirits separate when we die. While the physical body is returned to the earth, they believe that the spirits go into the spiritual world. They believe that the spiritual world is divided into two sections. I would venture to guess their spiritual worlds are a representation of heaven and hell. The LDS belief is that the spiritual world is separated into the spirit paradise and spirit prison. The reasoning is that, when someone dies, their spirits are sorted by how they lived their lives on earth. Spirit paradise is a place where the good spirits go to rest while they reunite with their family members who have passed, and wait for the rest of their family to join them.

On the one hand, you have the people who lived a good life, were good to others, and served God—who go to rest in spirit paradise. On the other hand, you have those who did not perform or act according to the prescribed word from the *Book of Mormon*—who get sent to spirit prison. The members of the LDS believe that the spirits that end up in spirit prison are given the chance to learn the gospel according to Jesus Christ. When they have learned all that they have needed to learn to ensure redemption, they will be given the chance to repent for their sins. This redemption will ultimately give them a pass to enter the spirit paradise, where they can rest until the day of judgment.

### Jehovah's Witness Church

The Jehovah's Witness church is a mainstream religious denomination that has many followers from all around the world. The members of the church believe that the body and the soul die when a person reaches the end of their life on earth. The church teaches its followers that death is the opposite of life. I do believe everyone will agree with that statement. The church also teaches that people who have passed away cannot hear, see, or think because their souls have died. Members of the Jehovah's Witness church will not entertain the idea of adding a bit of 'fantasy' for those who mourn their loved ones, because they are adamant that nothing survives when we die. The church doesn't seem to agree with science, medicine, and other religious denominations that believe that the body, soul, and spirit are separated at death.

## Moving Along: Author's Thoughts

I chose to highlight a couple of the religious denominations. I didn't do it to pick on any of the religious organizations. I wanted to show my readers what other churches believe. I am not in the business of running anyone down for their beliefs. I am fascinated by the different beliefs. I am not bothered by your gender, ethnicity, or which religious or non-religious path you follow. I want to know what is going on in people's minds, and how they think. I also want to share how people may choose to open the line of communication with their loved ones.

### Communicating With Your Dearly Departed

You have seen three different religious denominations mentioned in this chapter. Everyone who believes that Jesus Christ died on the cross and was resurrected is called a Christian. Not all religions believe in the afterlife, nor do they believe in communicating with their loved ones who have passed away. Most Christian religious denominations do believe that one can communicate with those who have left this world. The types of communication I have read about vary from person to person. I will share a couple of the communication methods that I have observed, or that I have read or been told about.

- Lighting candles

- Writing letters

- Singing and dancing

- Reading scripture from the Bible

- Praying

- Engaging in a one-sided conversation

- Intercessory prayers

You may be wondering where the other religions are, and what their beliefs are. Of course, the naysayers are smirking because they are preparing to write a review by accusing me of being biased. Sorry naysayers, I am one step ahead of you. Follow the Oreo cookie crumbs as I lead you into Chapter 4 where, would you believe, I will be speaking about the history of certain religions and ancient civilizations. I believe that the ancient civilizations and other religions needed their own chapter. I would label it as me being respectful. Come on everyone; it is time to dive into Chapter 4 with me.

Chapter 4:

# The History of Various

# Religious Beliefs and Practices

My fascination with this history of religions took me through many dark and dusty tunnels of the archives. A quick glance at the archives will reveal that religion stems back to many different civilizations dating back to a time before the birth of Jesus Christ. Many of these civilizations are still active, although more modern, and continue to worship a deity that is sacred to them. Everyone, across all religions and faiths, worships their deities by dancing, singing, and even praying. It is evident, when looking at the means of communication, that every religion or faith uses dancing, singing, chanting, and even praying as a means to interact with their god or loved ones.

Everyone wants to communicate with their deity of choice for personal reasons. Some may ask for favorable weather as they prepare to travel across the oceans. Others may ask for peace and reconciliation in countries that are devastated by wars or conflicts. Desperate times call for desperate measures, and people fall to their knees to pray for the health of their loved ones who are ill or dying. Some may find themselves at a crossroads in their lives, and may need guidance on where to go next. I find that I am closest to God when I am out cycling. That is when I can hear Him the loudest because I am not attached to a digital distraction. I'm not going to say that everyone will have the same experience, but everyone spends their time in praise and worship in whatever way fits their lifestyle.

One of the key takeaways of this book is that you are going to take everything that you have learned and store it in a safe place for future use. It is perfectly okay if you don't want to believe in what this book is about. One day your curiosity might be ignited when you are presented with a series of unexplained events. I have done all the research, as you have seen in previous chapters, so that you will have everything you need at your fingertips.

This chapter is all about the various civilizations, and how they perceive death, and the afterlife. The information is considered to be history because some of the beliefs may have changed to adapt to modern times. I will be sharing information about current religious groups and their beliefs. The trails through the past will direct you to the present.

# Modern-Day Religious Beliefs and Practices

There is a whole world beyond the many different Christian religious denominations and beliefs, as mentioned in Chapter 3. Every religion has beliefs that may not align with your beliefs. I wanted to separate the Christian religious denominations from the older religions that have their own version of God. This decision was not based on or backed by any bias. It is meant as a sign of respect for other religions. I didn't want to squeeze them in where they could be overlooked and dismissed by people who don't agree with their beliefs. I hope that you will continue reading and not skip over this chapter. I may have mentioned it a couple of times, and I may repeat it a couple more, but I am fascinated by all religions. I feel that by taking the time to understand other religions, I can connect with people more by showing them the respect that they deserve.

I have previously mentioned that the physical body is a temporary vessel that houses our souls and spirits. It is on loan to us for the duration of our stay on this earth. Our bodies are returned to the earth when our souls and spirits are separated, upon our death. We are tasked with the responsibility of taking care of our bodies. I needed to add this little reminder, here, as we explore the beliefs of other religions and civilizations. The communication methods of the following two modern-day religions are not mentioned; it is believed that communication may mimic those of the Christian faith. It is also believed that the members of the Hindu religion, and the Muslim faith, speak to their ancestors when they pray three times a day.

# The Hindu Religion

It is considered a tradition for members of the Hindu religion to die at home, surrounded by loved ones. It is not always possible to uphold the tradition, but it is adhered to, depending on the circumstances. After the death of loved ones, the family and community jump into action to start planning the funeral. Hindu funerals take place within 24 hours after the passing of the loved one. The idea behind the hasty funeral is to help the soul find its next vessel. Family members will assist with preserving the body until the funeral, and before the soul is reincarnated. They will wash and anoint the body, they will tie the thumbs and big toes together to keep the limbs in place, and they will dress their loved ones in clean clothes and wrap them in a cloth.

Members of the Hindu religion are cremated. Hindus will mourn their loved ones for anywhere between 10 to 13 days. This is the prescribed grieving period, but we all know that grief does not have a timetable. Everyone grieves differently, but I do believe that the 10 to 13 days mourning period is a sign of respect to the dearly departed and their family.

Members of the Hindu religion believe that the souls of every person on this earth are immortal and will live on in eternity. I previously mentioned the cycle of life, and that it is something that everyone goes through. The Hindus believe that the souls of people who have died are reincarnated, and the cycle of life starts over. One would almost say that our lifecycle is stuck in a time loop that keeps on going around to restart the cycle. This time loop is known as the *samsara* in the Hindu religion.

# The Islamic Faith

Members of the Islamic faith believe that Allah will determine when someone dies. It is also believed that the soul separates from the body when someone dies. Another belief is that the person who has passed away will be judged by Allah on the Day of Judgment. This means that they believe that the person who died will remain in their grave until the day that Allah recalls them to evaluate how they lived their life. I believe that this is a gentle reminder for people from all religions, and walks of life, to be kind and to do good things.

Members of the Islamic faith believe that the afterlife has 14 different stages. What we may call the afterlife, or life after death, is known as the *Akhirah*. Let's explore a couple of these stages.

## Barzakh

Barzakh refers to the status of the soul when the physical body dies. In layman's terms, Barzakh is when the soul waits for Allah to call it for the Day of Judgment. Some people also refer to Barzkh as the threshold between the physical world and the afterlife.

## Sounding of the Trumpet

Members of the Islamic faith believe that the angel, Hazrat Israfel, will blow the trumpet twice. The sounding trumpet will awaken the souls and they will follow angel Hazrat Israfel to the gathering place where they will wait for Allah. This stage of the afterlife is believed to be the start of the apocalypse, or Soor.

## The Apocalypse

The Merriam-Webster online dictionary tells us that the definition of the apocalypse stems from Christian and Jewish scripture. It is also believed to be something that is seen as a revelation as predicted by a prophecy. The apocalypse is described as being a cosmic catastrophe where God, Allah, Jehovah, or whichever deity you believe in, will rid the world of evil. A new world will be created where everyone will live a righteous life (Merriam-Webster, n.d.-a).

Members of the Islamic faith believe that one of the stages of the afterlife is called the apocalypse. Where the definition in the previous paragraph refers to a catastrophic event, the Islamic teaching of the apocalypse refers to the awakening of the people that have died. They will walk towards the place where all the dead people will wait for the arrival of Allah.

## The Resurrection

Members of the Islamic faith are taught that the resurrection could occur in different ways. One such teaching explains that those who have passed away will be lifted from their graves. They will be led to Allah, who will then judge them based on how they lived their lives and treated others in the physical world. Members of the Islamic faith believe that Allah is the only one that can raise someone's body and spirit.

## The Gathering Place

This is a stage that has been mentioned multiple times: the gathering place. Based on what has previously been said, the gathering place is where the souls that have been resurrected gather. It is at this gathering place that the resurrected souls will be given the Book of Deeds.

## The Book of Deeds

The souls that are at the gathering place are given the Book of Deeds. It is believed that the Book of Deeds is a record that has the names of everyone who has died. Each person who is recorded in the Book of Deeds has a list of everything, good and bad, that they have done during their cycle of life. The resurrected souls of the Islamic faith will have the opportunity to revisit the good and bad that they have done in their lifetime on earth.

## The Reckoning

Revisiting the Book of Deeds will help the resurrected souls reassess their transgressions before judgment is handed down.

## The Scale

All transgressions and good deeds are weighed during the next stage of the afterlife journey. A soul that carries more good than bad will receive its reprieve, and earn a pass to salvation. The soul whose bad deeds weigh more than the good deeds is sent to hell to suffer a punishment. Members of the Islamic faith believe that the souls that are sent to hell and complete their punishment will join the good souls in paradise.

## The River and the Pool of Kawthar

The Pool of Kawthar is the catchment area for the water that flows through the river of Paradise. The pool appears on the Day of Judgment. All the souls of the resurrected men are gathered at the pool, alongside Prophet Hazrat Muhammad. Members of the Islamic faith believe that the first soul to reach the pool will become a prophet.

## The Sirat

The bridge that spans from hell to paradise is called the Sirat. All resurrected souls have to cross the bridge. Every resurrected soul that steps onto the bridge is weighed, based on the good and the bad that they have done during their lifetime, which also determines the speed at which they will cross the bridge.

## Intercession

This stage of the journey to the afterlife could be labeled as the 'desperate' stage. This is the stage where the resurrected souls that had more sins than are allowed start begging for forgiveness. They will ask everyone to beg for forgiveness. It is also believed that the people who do not have any sin will also beg for assistance to be moved to a higher level within the afterlife.

## Purgatory

Another name for purgatory in the Islamic faith is Araf. It is believed that Araf is the threshold that separates paradise and hell. All the resurrected souls stand at the threshold and wait for Allah to decide who gets to go where.

## Hell

I do believe that everyone knows what hell is. Whether it truly exists is open for interpretation. The Bible, as we know it, does not refer to hell by name. Members of the Islamic faith believe that hell is where the souls who have accumulated the worst deeds go. It is believed that the souls that enter hell are punished and tortured, based on their transgressions. This type of punishment is known as Jahannam in the Islamic faith, and the most common form of torture is being burned by fire.

## Paradise

The last and final stage of the journey to reach the afterlife is when the resurrected souls enter paradise. This is the place everyone on earth needs to aim for. The price to get into paradise is not going to break the bank. All it is going to take is being a good person, having good morals, and being the kind of person that does good in the world. I believe that paradise is what heaven is like. No one will experience sadness; all the aches, pains, and diseases will be washed away; and the elements of nature will not be a problem.

# Ancient Civilizations Beliefs and Practices

The research I have done about the beliefs, rituals, and practices of the various religions, religious denominations, and ancient civilizations has tickled my curiosity. I may have mentioned a couple of times that I am fascinated by the thought that there is a life after this one. I have an insatiable curiosity that needs to know more, as well as understand what my ancestors believed about death and the afterlife. I know that some of the rituals, beliefs, and practices that take place in modern-day religions may raise an eyebrow or three across the board. I also know that some of the modern-day religious beliefs, rituals, and practices do not align with what more traditional religions and religious denominations believe.

I'm not here to approve or dispute any of the beliefs, rituals, and practices of others. Every bit of research I am doing just adds a little more fuel to my fire. Everything I am learning increases the fire in my soul to want to know more. I have heard that curiosity may have killed the cat, but I can assure you that this is not going to be my fate. The curiosity in me is growing increasingly stronger, the further along I progress with this journey. Come on, hop into the time portal with me. We are going to take a jump back in time to see what the ancient civilizations have to say about the death of people, and the afterlife.

## *Ancient Aztec*

Mesoamerica was home to the Aztec population during the period ranging from the 14th to the 16th centuries. Today, Mesoamerica is known as Mexico, which has become a favorite holiday destination of millions. It is rumored that the ancient Aztec civilization was resourceful and skilled, and boasted about their accomplishments relating to architecture, language, farming, and many others. As much as I would love to share everything about this fascinating civilization, we are here to learn about their beliefs, practices, and rituals about the death of loved ones.

The ancient Aztec civilization is notoriously recognized for its religion. Their religious practices included mass sacrifices of thousands of people. It is believed that the Aztecs ventured outside of their camps to seek more people to sacrifice. Mass sacrifices were performed to keep the ancestors and deities happy. They believed that it was their duty to keep the spirits and gods well-nourished. The reward would then be a healthy, happy, and well-balanced universe.

The ancient Aztec civilization's view of the afterlife differs from what we have learned from other religions. Most religions believe that the fate of someone's afterlife is based on how they lived their life. The Aztecs believe that their place in the afterlife would be determined by the way they died. Where the Islamic faith has different stages that lead to the final resting place, the ancient Aztec civilization has different heavens. Each of the heavens has specific requirements for entry.

- Soldiers who perished during a battle or were sacrificed are sent to a heaven in the east, where the sun rises in the morning.

- The death of a woman during childbirth is believed to be an act of bravery that sees her being sent to a heaven in the west, where the sun sets in the evening.

- People who have lost their lives due to natural disasters such as drowning, certain diseases, or acts of violence are sent to Tlalocan, which is one of the 13 heavens being guarded by Tlaloc.

Let's flip the coin to find out the fate of those who didn't make it to one of the heavens to live happily ever after. People who died of 'normal' deaths, such as diseases that are not considered to be part of nature or old age, were sent to a place by the name of Mictlan. I would assume that Mictlan, which is in the underworld, is the same as the version of hell that we are familiar with. It is believed that the souls that were sent to Mictlan had to endure various obstacles as they descended from the top level, to the ninth level, to their destination.

Family members would include items of importance in their burial sites of the 'normal' deaths. This was done so that they could remember the type of lives they lived when they were in the underworld. However, if someone died of a noble death, such as fighting in a battle, the wife of that person would be buried alive. This was done to prove her loyalty to her husband. The same fate would be applicable if that man had a slave.

## *Ancient Egyptians*

The next stop on our time travel journey takes us to the ancient land of pyramids. The ancient Egyptians believed that when someone died, their death was to be celebrated. They would be treated with respect and sent off to the next life with dignity. We have to remember that women living in ancient times were not considered to be equal to their counterparts. It was the women's duty to perform rituals when their loved ones had passed on. They would walk around in public areas and show their distress by chanting and beating their chests, while covered in mud. It is believed that wealthy families would hire mourners to act distressed.

The bodies of the loved ones that had died had to be embalmed, or mummified, so that they would be protected from decay. The ancient Egyptians believed that it was important to mummify the bodies and preserve them so that they would enjoy eternal life. The proper procedures of a burial need to take place. The ancient Egyptians believed that the ghost of their loved ones would linger if the burial was not done correctly. Only once the bodies were laid to rest in their coffins, and sealed in the tombs, could the lives of the dearly departed be celebrated.

The ancient Egyptian afterlife procedure closely resembles that of the Islamic faith. The beliefs, rituals, and practices of the ancient civilizations were in place before many of the more modern-day religions. They may seem similar, yet they are different. Every religion, whether ancient or modern, deserves to be respected for setting the standards for demanding respect for their dearly departed. I know that many of them may seem archaic and cruel, but I do believe that there is a method behind their madness.

Loved ones believed that they could communicate with their dearly departed by way of the mortuary chapel. The ancient beliefs were that the spirits of those that had passed on would leave the tomb through a false door. This would allow the spirits to take up residence in one of the statues of a deceased person. Loved ones would take food, drinks, and items of importance as an offering to their dearly departed. Ancient Egyptian families had a responsibility to their loved ones in the afterlife, and that was to ensure that their tombs were well taken care of. The tombs were decorated with drawings and inscriptions, which would be identified as afterlife directions for when the families were no longer able to fulfill their roles as caretakers.

## *The Hall of Truths*

The souls that are separated from their physical bodies go to the Hall of Truths. They form an assembly line where they wait for the god of the afterlife, Osiris, to tell them their fate. Osiris is joined by 42 judges, who will read through a list that contains 42 sins that may have been committed against the gods, strangers, or family. The 42 judges are allegedly referred to as the negative confessions, which are used as an indicator to test whether a person was guilty of any transgressions. The judges may as well be referred to as the lie detectors of the soul, and any soul that is believed to be lying will be reported to the district judge, who in this scenario is Osiris.

An in-depth discussion takes place between the Osiris and the judges, where all the souls are judged based on their confessions. The confessions or transgressions are weighed on a scale by using a rather unique formula. On the one side of the scale, they have the truth feather. This feather weighs the heart of the soul that is waiting to find out its fate. If the heart weighs less than the feather, the soul will be transported to the afterlife. Should the soul's heart weigh more than the feather, then that soul is found guilty of transgressions. Some religions believe that the bad souls will go to hell, or live in a place where they will suffer for all eternity. The ancient Egyptian civilizations don't believe in hell. I would like to believe that they wouldn't want any bad souls to linger around while good souls are living in a peaceful paradise. The ancient Egyptians believe that the blackened souls will have their hearts ripped out and thrown on the ground. Their hearts will be eaten by creatures, or cleaners, that rid the afterlife of bad souls.

### The Field of Reeds

The ancient Egyptian afterlife is known as the Field of Reeds. I just have to look at the name, and I am imagining a very beautiful place where everyone is carefree and enjoying the peace and serenity of their new place of residence. However, the new residents have a little obstacle course they need to participate in before they reach the Field of Reeds. Their trek to their final resting place will first take them to Lily Lake. This trek to Lily Lake is dependent on the type of life they lived based on their health, physical problems, or perhaps even being bullied. No two souls will experience the same obstacles. It is also not a race to see who will get to Lily Lake first.

The souls are met by a ferryman who will safely transport them to the Field of Reeds when they have overcome their obstacles. It is believed, as I had imagined, that the Field of Reeds is a beautiful place that may resemble a favorite home they once resided in. The new souls will be greeted by their loved ones, pets, and anyone who may have joined the afterlife before them. It is here, in the Field of Reeds, that the ancient Egyptians believed that they would spend all of eternity.

## *Moving Along: Author's Thoughts*

I hope that you have found this chapter as fascinating as I have. The world of religion, whether modern or ancient civilizations, has many beliefs and rituals. I would be writing about all the different beliefs, and never get to answer what I asked when I started this book.

I am going to be dedicating the next chapter to all the amazing humans that deal with the end of life. This is a daily occurrence for them, which they take in their stride. If it were not for these amazing humans, those that are left behind would not cope with the pressures that the death of loved ones, or beloved pets, bring. They help the weak to be strong. They give us hope that, one day, everyone will be together.

Do I still believe that there is a life after this one? Absolutely. There is no doubt in my mind that I will be met by Dad, Amadeus, and all my ancestors. See you in the next chapter.

# Chapter 5:

# Heroes of Their Profession—

# True Life Angels

The job market consists of many professions. Every profession is made up of special people who know how to sell or do what they need to. Every person enters that profession for a reason. I believe in being in the right place at the right time, and doing the right thing. I know, and acknowledge, that this is an unpopular belief that is not supported by many. I also know that many will tell me where to shove my beliefs, because they are settling for jobs that are nowhere near their qualifications. Every job requires someone with special skills. No matter which profession you find yourself in, it is where you are meant to be. The purpose may not be known to you, but you have to believe that there is one.

We take a lot for granted. We are quick to criticize this one and that one for how they do their job. We should be saying *thank you*. Yes, we should even thank the annoying telemarketer who reads from a script to try and sell us whatever is on their agenda for the day. You may be talking to the person you are meant to inspire and uplift. We don't know what goes on in the lives of those who work 12-hour shifts, or what they have to endure to take home a paycheck at the end of each week or month.

# The Dedication

I would like to dedicate the rest of this chapter to the true-life angels of their professions. I believe that they are superheroes who do not get enough recognition for what they do. I would like to place these professions on a pedestal because they deal with more than anyone may realize. I am speaking of professions that work with people who are dying and have died. These special people give us hope. They help us grieve the loss of our loved ones. They keep a flame of hope alive because they know how important it is to believe. This chapter is dedicated to doctors, nurses, morticians, graveyard diggers, crematorium workers, and so many more. Let's take a look at how some of these amazing people, in their chosen professions, experience the aftermath of what the death of a person may bring to their jobs.

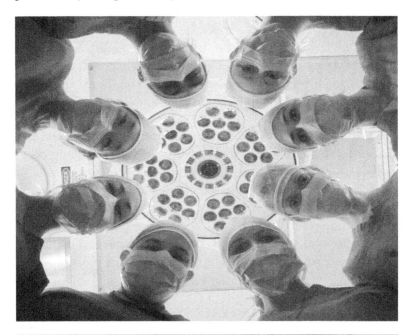

## *Through the Eyes of Doctors, Nurses, and Caregivers*

Doctors contribute to the life cycle of a human being. They are there when life begins, and they are there (mostly) when lives come to an end. I believe that members of the medical profession see and hear more than what they share with their families. Many would argue that if the patient said something, regardless of what it was, the family has a right to know what was said. Others would say that members of the medical profession want to protect the families from being hurt even more. I think that it is safe to say that everyone has an opinion, and it's okay to not be on the same page all the time.

I can't imagine the stress that gets piled onto the plates of doctors, nurses, and caregivers. I recently watched a short video about doctors who are forced to be the bearer of bad news to hopeful families. The families don't want to believe that their loved ones are most likely not going to leave the hospital. This is something that happens when a diagnosis is given, and the patients are told that they have six to twelve months to live. The patient ends up in the hospital, where they are not doing well. Trauma doctors are called in to speak to the families, only to realize that they have certain expectations. Hospice care is suggested, only to be shot down by family of patients, because they were told that they had time before the end of care would be necessary.

Death brings about many emotions. Some are not as pleasant as the movies or television shows would portray. People in the real world have issues. Each person that prepares to meet their maker will have a different experience. Let's take a look at a couple of examples that doctors and nurses experience during the final moments of their patient's life.

## Anger

Anger is a normal emotion that everyone experiences. Nurse Agnes tells us about a gang member who was in the final stages of his life. His loving and religious family members were gathered around his bed. His family was telling him that he would be okay, and that his transgressions would be forgiven in the afterlife. His mother, who thought that he was afraid to die, told him to walk toward Jesus who was waiting in the light. Nurse Agnes remembers his reaction, which she described as an anger she had never before experienced. She said that his eyes were black as coal. He shouted at his mother, and uttered very angry profanities which, when translated, told her to stick her light and Jesus where the sun doesn't shine. In the blink of an eye, the man screamed at something he had seen, and died. Nurse Agnes recalls that the man looked as though he was frozen in fear. His family was left astonished, and some were even afraid because they couldn't understand what had happened. What had he seen that had made him scream out in fear? Nurse Agnes, who had been around death for many years, believes that he saw his fate after the way he treated his religious mother.

## My Loved One Is Here

People will experience many things while standing at the threshold between the two worlds. Doctors and nurses share that they can predict when their patients are preparing to cross the threshold. A doctor remembers Mrs. Anderson. She was one of those patients that doctors, nurses, caregivers, and everyone that meets her falls in love with. She was always helping people where she could. She was the life of the room when she entered it, always greeting everyone by name, and saying something that would make the person feel special. As far as life goes, Mrs. Anderson was not getting any younger. She started spending more time in bed than in the communal lounge of the care home. The doctor visited Mrs. Anderson daily and, on one of his visits, she told him that she was aging gracefully and that her end was near. He laughed and told her that she would outlive everyone on the planet, to which she guffawed.

The doctor knew, the day that he entered Mrs. Anderson's room, that it was going to be her last. She opened her eyes as he walked in, and she smiled at him. She told him that she was very happy that he had come because she wanted to introduce him to James, her husband. The doctor knew that Mrs. Anderson's husband had passed away in the '80s, but he smiled and greeted James as if he could see him. He remembers smelling an aftershave that reminded him of his grandfather— the smell of Old Spice. Mrs. Anderson looked at her doctor and thanked him for always visiting. She told him that she appreciated his visits but it was time for him to spend less time visiting dying old ladies. She went on to tell him that his wife needed him, and his support, more than ever. The puzzled look on his face made her laugh, and she told him to go home and speak to his wife. The last thing she said to him was that James had bought the ticket for their trip, and it was time to leave. She closed her eyes, and let out a happy sigh as she expelled her last breath.

The doctor stayed with Mrs. Anderson until the funeral home arrived to fetch her body. He signed all the paperwork that needed to be signed. He had noticed that the smell of Old Spice had been replaced by vanilla and roses. The doctor finally left the care home with a heavy heart. His wife was waiting for him when he walked into his house. She had known how special Mrs. Anderson was to him. They sat in the kitchen as he shared the final moments with his patient. The kitchen smelled of vanilla and roses, and he looked around as he sniffed. His wife looked around to see what he was looking for. He asked her if she also smelled vanilla and roses, and she shook her head. He then remembered what Mrs. Anderson had told him about his wife needing his support. He asked his wife, and she smiled at him as she reached into her pocket, and pulled out a pregnancy test. How did Mrs. Anderson know? At their three-month doctor's visit, they found out that they were having twins. Again, the doctor could smell vanilla and roses. The doctor was convinced that Mrs. Anderson was his family's guardian angel. And no, if you were wondering, they didn't name their babies after Mr. and Mrs. Anderson.

## *Bone-Chilling Funeral Home Experiences*

The next stage, after death, is preparing for the funeral. The bodies of those that have crossed the threshold into the next life are sent to the funeral home. It is here that the bodies are prepared for burial or cremation. The curse of the curious mind doesn't have any boundaries. When the curious mind wants to know something, or write a book, some investigating has to happen. I needed to know if funeral homes could give me some insight. Who better to ask for help than someone who works with bodies? I wanted an answer to a question that I have been wondering about since I started on this journey. It was a question that no one other than the people who work in morgues or funeral homes would have an answer to. I want to know if any of the straggling souls had tried to communicate with the people in this profession. Let's take a look to see if my question can be answered.

## Organ Donations

A tissue recovery technician shares their experience of an incident that occurred early on in their career. Part of a tissue recovery technician's job is to prepare the bodies of those who had recently passed away. The bodies would still be warm to the touch when they were sent to the morgue. A technician's job is to prepare the body, and retrieve the tissue as soon as possible. The technician remembers the day they had their first encounter with someone in the afterlife. They were holding the hand of their patient, and speaking to them, as they gently started shaving the hair on their arm. The technician said that they always spoke to their patients because they were the best listeners. They said that while they were shaving the patient's arm, the body started going into rigor mortis. This is where the muscles in the body of the deceased person begin to stiffen. The technician felt the fingers of their patient start to wrap around their hand. They recall being alarmed, at first, because they had never had such an experience. The technician calmly continued with the task at hand, because time was of the essence. They did say that they felt calm as the patient 'held' their hand. When they had finished shaving the patient's arm, the hand opened and released the technician's hand. When the technician had completed the tissue retrieval, they did something that they had never done before, which was to lift the sheet that was covering their patient. What the technician saw brought them to tears. The patient was an elderly gentleman who had a smile on his face, and fresh tear tracks were also on his face.

The technician believed that the gentleman was overcome with gratitude that someone was treating his body with respect. They continued to speak to their patients while preparing them for the retrieval. They were not alarmed, nor afraid when someone held their hand, which seemed to happen often. The technician believed that everyone needed to be treated with respect, whether living or dead. They said that when someone who had crossed over wanted to hold their hand, and thank them for showing respect, they knew that they didn't have to be afraid.

### The Embalming Process

The next story comes from someone new to the embalming career. The embalmer starts by saying how excited they were to be in their chosen career. When asked if they were afraid to be alone in a room with dead bodies, their answer was *absolutely not*. They said that the only difference between people who were living and dead was that one group couldn't talk back and tell them that their singing was terrible. They were asked if they had any encounters with any of the patients that had passed on. One of their earliest encounters with things that went bump in the dark was on a day when they were working the night shift. No one else was inside the building—or so they thought. They remember going to the restroom, and then returning to the "beauty salon" to start preparing a body for burial. Before they got to the "beauty salon", they heard what sounded like a lady sobbing, and feet shuffling on the floor. They said it sounded as if the person was dragging their feet as they moved around.

The embalmer followed the sounds, and almost expected to find that a loved one had walked in to spend the last moments with their dearly departed. It was known to have happened before. The sobbing and shuffling led the embalmer to a room where the prepared bodies were waiting to be transported to their burial. The embalmer looked around the room to determine if they could see the grieving family member, but the room was empty of any living bodies. However, in the corner of the room was only one body. The body belonged to a young girl who had taken her life. They believed that the young girl was trying to tell her family that she was sorry for putting them through the heartbreak they were experiencing. The embalmer also knew that the young girl would be sticking around until she had made peace with what she had done to herself.

The embalmer was asked if they were afraid when they heard the sobbing and shuffling. Their response was *no*, they were not afraid. They believed that the funeral home was a gathering site for straggler souls that hadn't left because they were waiting for their loved ones to join them. The embalmer said that they had names for all the bumps, bangs, clatters, and rattles that they heard while they were working. They believed that every little sound that echoed through the quiet room was one of the stragglers. Some even liked to brush past them to make their presence known. Another soul was a notorious prankster who would open the snack drawer in the kitchen and move the snacks around.

## *The Great Afterlife Debate Continues: Author's Thoughts*

This chapter has been about sharing experiences of the people who either deal with death, or dead bodies. These are the people who flit around and do what needs to be done, calmly. These are the people who have respect for their charges, regardless of the role they play at whatever stage of life or death. The internet is full of forums where people share their experiences. I needed to share a couple of the stories I found, and add my interpretation of the events.

I have heard people say that they are afraid of death. They don't know what is waiting for them. They don't know if all communication channels will fail to work. They don't know if they can look down on their loved ones who have been left behind. This book is all about looking for the answers to those questions. I don't know what's waiting beyond the threshold. No one knows until they get there.

I spoke to a retired caregiver, and asked for her views regarding life after death. This is the story of Sandy, the lady who promised to let her caregiver know that she was popping in as she had promised: "I have always been the type of person to do the right thing. I believed that my main purpose on this earth was to make sure that everyone around me was taken care of. That is why I became a caregiver. I started my caregiving career by looking after children. I then moved on to taking care of elderly people. The lady I was working for, Sandy, was an extremely kind soul. She always told me that she would find a way to let me know that she was around. I always laughed her off. Sandy passed away a couple of years later. One day, not too long after Sandy's passing, I was having a really hard day. My husband was away on a business trip, and I felt all alone. I was sitting at my kitchen table and feeling rather sad for myself. I felt a cool wisp of air around me. The windows were closed. The next moment I was smelling a perfume that I had only ever come across once before. I sat up, and looked around. I stood up, prepared two cups of tea and a plate of shortbread, and set it down on the table. I knew, without a shadow of a doubt, that Sandy had popped in for a cup of tea. She said that she would find a way to let me know she was around, and she didn't lie."

Come on, follow me as we dive into the next chapter. I'll protect you from your fears. Stay close at all times.

# Chapter 6:

# Exploring Communication Channels—When to Connect with the Dearly Departed

I remember a youth pastor from one of the mainstream churches telling youngsters to put their mobile phones into a box. Those that are familiar with teenagers will agree that asking them to put their phones away for longer than five minutes equates to their world falling apart. I would also add that many adults are not far behind the teenagers. Everyone is so invested in what is happening on social media, that they are afraid to sleep at night for fear of missing something important. I believe that everyone who has ever had some form of an electronic device is guilty of this 'addiction.'

The youth pastor spoke to the group of sulking teenagers, who were most likely contemplating leaving, and never returning. He showed his young audience that he wasn't affected by their attitudes after their lifelines and extra limbs were removed. He asked a couple of questions, but there was one specific question that stood out to me. I believe that this is a question that should be printed on the packaging of all electronic devices. *What are you going to do with your phone when you are dead?*

We invest so much of our time and money in these devices. I have witnessed many *anything you can do, I can do better* moments, when it comes to phones. It is a constant competition to see who has the best phone, who has the most storage space, or who can take the most selfies. What is the purpose? The youth pastor asked one of the teenagers if he had God as a contact on his phone, or whether he chatted to God on messages, WhatsApp, or FaceTime. The young man looked at the Youth Pastor as if he had lost a couple of marbles. What good is a phone if you can't use it to communicate with people who are no longer living in this world?

I know my naysayers are going to come at me. They may just refer to me as the Pied Piper of vulnerable and grieving people who are going to lead them to whatever version of hell they believe in. I have reached the point in my life where I don't care what others think about me. I know what I am doing, and I know that I have the answers I have been yearning for. I know that nothing in this life is guaranteed. I believe that we live in a world that is oozing with so much hate, conflict, anger, and everything negative. We have forgotten how to be nice to others, accepting that not everyone expects something in return for doing a good deed, or using a smile to touch someone's soul.

## Afterlife Direct

Thank you for calling Afterlife Direct. Please stick around for the options (questions) that will follow. We will attempt to answer your pressing questions in a timely manner. We, here at Afterlife Direct, value your time, patience, and understanding. We hope you have a blessed day.

- Does communication have to be at a designated place: such as a church, or the graveyard?

- Does communication have to take place at a specific time of day: such as midnight, or the time that the loved one left the physical world?

- Does communication have to take place on a certain day: such as a full moon, or an anniversary/birthday of the loved one?

- Are sacrifices required for communication to be effective?

- Is special clothing required for communication to be effective?

- Who provides the recipe to make the potion that is required for the communication to be effective?

I know that some of these questions may seem slightly juvenile. I am hoping that I have given everyone a reason to smile and eased their anxiety, that may be at an uncomfortable level. However, these types of questions have been asked. Looking at these questions fills me with sadness. Communication with the living is easy. You pick up your phone, punch in some numbers, press call, and wait for someone to pick up. Why can't communication with our dearly departed be as easy? I know that many articles and books have been written about how our loved ones communicate with us. I even have a section in my previous book about how our loved ones communicate with us. It is not as easy to spot the signs that alert us that someone is trying to communicate. Oh yes, the feathers and butterflies are easy enough to spot, but what about other types of signs that have not yet been documented?

## *Exploring Communication Channels*

Let's push the elephant out of the room by answering your questions in one swoop. I am pretty confident that you don't, won't, and never will need anything prefaced with 'special' to communicate with your dearly departed. The recipe for a successful communication channel is to have an open mind, add in a dash of hope, a teaspoon of belief, and a cup of love. Mix the four ingredients together, and rely on your senses to intercept messages that are meant for you. The messages I am referring to are signs that would let you know that your loved ones are trying to communicate with you.

Some people may require the help of a professional to guide them through the initial process. Some people may want to be left alone to contemplate their options. Some people will want to start exploring the different communication channels as soon as possible. It is important to remember that one size doesn't fit all. One person's choice of communication may not work for others. Every person has to find a method that works for them.

### *Prayer*

I believe that praying is one of the best, and most successful, communication channels available. You've heard of breakfast on the run—here you have praying on the run. Prayer is an open-ended conversation between you and your deity of choice. Prayer doesn't require any skills, or bargaining tools: "If you do this, then I will…" You can sing your prayers, you can pray out loud, or you can say it in your mind. All prayers are heard, even if you don't feel that way. This might be a difficult concept to understand, but what seems like forever on earth in the blink of an eye for God. Time moves a little differently in heaven than it does on earth. I like to think that God is giving us the time and space to develop patience and build up our faith. I believe, without a doubt, that God will never forsake us in our time of need.

Someone shared their prayer experience with me, and I must admit that I was excited for this person. They told me that they had been having a really difficult time focusing on life because the longing for their dearly departed was weighing them down. They would go to bed at night and sob until they fell asleep. On the third night of sobbing and longing, they decided to change their evening prayer routine. They thanked God for the lovely day, and for helping them get through the day. They prayed for everyone and everything on their prayer list. They got to the end of their prayer, hesitated, and then asked God if He could send their loved one for a visit. They said that they didn't want to have a conversation, or see them; all that they wanted was to feel their loved one's presence. They ended the prayer and lay in darkness, as the tears continued to flow. They said that they felt the movement at the corner of the bed, close to their head. They remember feeling the mattress sink, as if someone was sitting down. They then said that they felt as if someone was covering them with a blanket, and tucking them in. The tears stopped flowing, as they felt calm and peaceful.

## Séance

You will receive no judgment from me if you don't believe that praying is an effective communication channel. It is important to remember that someone who is grieving may not find the solace in religion that someone else has. It is also important that those who are grieving not be forced into a corner, or given something that resembles an ultimatum. It is not your duty to tell others who and what they should believe in. It is, however, your duty as friends or loved ones to show your support to those who are feeling the loss of their loved ones.

Grieving loved ones may have questions. Maybe they want closure that their dearly departed have settled in wherever they are. Maybe they want to know that they have been forgiven. Maybe they want to know if they have reconnected with Aunt Pearl, and whether she has shared her snickerdoodle recipe. Maybe they want to know where the gold bars have been hidden. The grieving loved ones decide to call in the help of someone, whether it is a clairvoyant or a medium, to help them communicate with their dearly departed. The clairvoyant or medium will relay questions or messages from the dearly departed. An ideal setting to host a séance would be to have a minimum of three people in a packed auditorium. Everyone is asked to have an open mind, because you don't want someone who is going to be negative and thwart your attempts at getting the closure that you need.

I was introduced to a well-known psychic medium, Theresa Caputo, while watching an episode of the *Kelly Clarkson Show*. Caputo hails from a show by the name of *Long Island Medium* on the *TLC* network. Clarkson and her stylist, Candace, sit down with Caputo for a conversation. Caputo asks who had recently lost a mother-like figure, and Candace acknowledges the question. She continues asking questions, which I would believe are to ascertain that she is the person the departed soul is trying to connect with. Caputo asks Candace if she was watching her mother's breath as she left the physical world, and once Candace has confirmed, Caputo tells her that her mother knows how much her daughter misses her. The questions continue, lots of tears are spilled, and much was said to convince Candace, and Clarkson, that spirits do see everything that we do. At one point, Caputo asks Candace about a blanket. Candace gasps and admits that she stole a blanket so that she could stay close to her mother.

Not everyone may get the answers that they are looking for when they perform séances. I have watched quite a few of the psychic mediums—which include John Edward, Derren Brown, Theresa Caputo, and many others—to understand that they are trying to get us to see and understand. One thing that I have learned is that you may not hear from the one person you wanted to contact. I believe that, if you are going to have a séance, invite a medium over to do a reading, or consult your ouija board, then you have to be prepared for the unexpected.

## From the Pen of John Allen: An Emotional Encounter

During the summer of 2014, friends let me know that they were going to be in North Carolina visiting family. We made plans to meet up on a Friday night. It was a lovely, relaxing evening. We spent hours talking about our families, friends, work, and just everything that could be crammed into a visit where everyone was in the loop of what was going on.

These friends, who have since moved to Italy, had experienced heartbreak when they lived in North Carolina. They lost their only son, Luka, in a freak swimming accident off the North Carolina coast in 2011. I know how hard it was to lose a parent, but I can't even begin to imagine how anyone would feel losing a child. I have always heard parents say that they shouldn't be burying their children, because they still have a whole lifetime of good to do.

Our evening came to an end after we may or may not have consumed way too much delicious food and desserts, and enjoyed a couple of belly laughs. I arrived home around midnight but, instead of going to bed, I found myself going to the lounge and plopping down on the sofa. I may have blamed the good food and company for my laziness to go up to my bedroom. I didn't bother turning the lights on, and sat in the dark with my thoughts. My mind was working through the evening, when out of nowhere, I thought about Luka. I was thinking about the tragedy that had claimed his life at such a young age. I don't know what prompted me, but I called out: "Luka, if you are here with me now, please give me a sign." I honestly had no expectations of what may or may not happen. The next moment, I felt an icy breeze on the back of my neck. I looked around my dark living room to see if maybe the window was open, but it was not. I looked up at the ceiling to see if the fan was on, but it was not. There were no logical explanations as to how an icy breeze could blow on my neck. Was I afraid? No, I was not. Who or what could it have been? Was it possible that perhaps Luka had answered my call?

The next morning, Saturday, I was out in the backyard doing some weeding and cleaning. The events of the previous evening had been shoved to the back burner while I tackled my weekend chores. The next moment, out of nowhere, I spotted a huge black butterfly who seemed to be on a mission to use my face as its target practice. I stepped back and did a *Matrix* move to prevent the butterfly from making contact with my face. I watched it for a while as it fluttered around my garden— possibly ensuring that I was doing a good job. It flew up, went over the fence, and into the neighbors' yard. I was rooted to the spot because, believe it or not, in the eight years that I had been living in my house, I had never seen a butterfly. I continued with my task of cleaning and ridding the backyard of weeds.

Later in the afternoon, I received a text from my friends to say that their plans for the evening had been canceled. They asked if I would like to join them for dinner again that night. Hello, I'm always up for a good meal and great company, so naturally I responded with a *yes*. We had a lovely time together again, talking, eating, and there may have been a bottle of wine between us. Towards the end of the meal, I had built up the courage to tell them what had happened when I got home the previous evening. I told them everything, from calling out Luka's name and feeling the icy breeze on my neck, to almost being the black butterfly's target practice that morning.

My friend started to cry, and the guilt I felt was like a wave crashing over me. At that point, I wished I had kept my mouth closed. My friend then reached down to their handbag, and pulled out a photograph that they handed to me. I looked at the photograph, and stared at it in shock. It was a photo of Luka, and on his outstretched hand was a giant black butterfly. I think the air was knocked out of me, because I couldn't say anything or do anything.

- Had I contacted Luka?

- Was the icy breeze on my neck a sign that Luka was there?

- Was the giant black butterfly Luka?

- Was Luka letting me know that he was around me?

I can tell you that I lived in that house for 15 years. That was the first and last time I had ever seen a butterfly at the house. Do I believe that it was Luka? *Oh yes, I do believe that it was.* I will repeat what I said in the previous section: everyone can be a psychic. All it takes is an—say it with me—open mind!

Chapter 7:

# Using Technology to Interact

# With Straggling Souls

I have dedicated the first six chapters of this book trying to prove that communication with the dearly departed is possible. I have dragged you around dusty archives, through a couple of ancient civilizations, and taken you to hear some personal accounts relating to various communication experiences. Everything that has been covered has been referenced to religion, beliefs, and/or practices. Many of my critics are most likely wielding crosses to exorcise the 'evil' that they believe is hiding between the pages. I have a couple of questions for those who want to burn me at the stake.

- Have you ever watched movies, television shows, or documentaries that centered around ghosts or evil spirits (demons)?

- Have you ever read ghost stories?

- Have you ever been able to find out why your television or radio turns on when you are the only one in the house?

- Have you ever wondered why you get goose flesh, or why the hair on the back of your neck or arms stands to attention, for no reason?

- Do you have an explanation for things that go bump in the night?

If you have answered yes to one of these questions, you may be mildly curious about what happens on the other side of the threshold. If you have answered yes to more than one of these questions, then I would respectfully request that you put your crosses of condemnation, and judgment, away. I would like to invite you to join me as we learn, together, how modern technology can provide the proof you don't want to believe is true.

I don't know why straggling souls remain earthbound. I don't know what they went through during their time on this earth. I don't know how to communicate with the souls of people I am not familiar with. I have watched many documentaries and shows about paranormal investigations. I researched whether paranormal investigators were a career option. I wanted to know whether these paranormal experts in their career fields could help with my questions.

- Why do straggler souls remain earthbound?

- Why are some straggler souls friendly?

- Why are some straggler souls malicious?

- How can we, normal people, know if straggler souls are around us?

Did you know that you have choices? You do, because I can clearly recall showing you how you could communicate with your loved ones. Communication with your loved ones is much easier than you may think. I do understand that you may be afraid to do it alone, and that is why I showed you that you could have a séance, a psychic medium, or a psychic that reads cards. Maybe the communication methods that have been shared are not entirely your cup of tea, and you would prefer to find alternative methods. Again, there is nothing wrong with that because you have choices. I want to introduce you to the world of paranormal experts. You can consult your local listings, or click on a couple of links, to find a professional expert. You can even choose to do it yourself by purchasing all the necessary gadgets.

# Looking Over the Shoulder of Paranormal Experts

I am going to introduce you to two gentlemen who founded The Atlantic Paranormal Society (TAPS) in 1990. TAPS was officially introduced to the viewing population across the globe in 2004. I will admit that it took me a while to get used to the idea that "ghost hunters" were real. I had always believed that people like Jason Hawes and Grant Wilson, who started *Ghost Hunters* in 2004, were actors in a new Science Fiction show on television. They worked as plumbers during the day, and exchanged their plumbing tools for ghost-hunting tools at night. It was their show that tickled my curiosity. After a couple of clicks here and a couple more there, I discovered that this whole ghost-hunting business was a blooming career for many. Their show, the *Ghost Hunters*, was the starting point for many other shows.

I watched a couple of the earlier episodes when *Ghost Hunters* premiered. I do remember that I was fascinated with their equipment, and how they would set up the place they were going to investigate. After speaking to the owner or host of the property, they would go in and lay cables and set up cameras. When everything was ready Jason, Grant, and their cameraman would prepare for whatever was waiting for them in the dark shadows of the place they were at. The lights would go out, and one would turn on his thermal camera, and the other would hold out his electronic voice phenomena (EVP) recorder. One of them would always have a thermometer to record sudden drops or spikes in temperature. I remember seeing them play tricks on each other, but I also remember moments when their cameraman picked up shadows or orbs. People were always on the fence about whether they were seeing footage that had been manipulated for the viewing pleasure of their audience. Maybe it was, maybe it wasn't; but, the consultation at the end of each show would make you rewind to see if you could hear what they were playing for the owner.

## *Budding Straggling Soul Communicator*

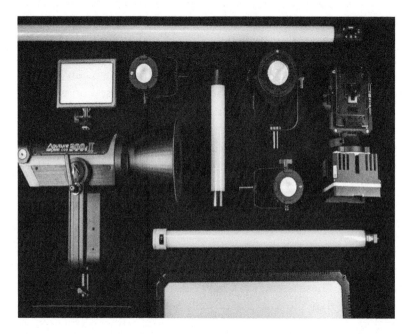

You may have opted to skip the professional ghost hunting experts—costs do tend to add up (or so I am told). You may believe that you can go to the local gadget store and purchase what you need. Right about now, your heart is probably trying to escape through your chest because you have an option that you hadn't considered. Your intuition censors are alerting the hairs on your arms and the back of your neck to prickle, as well as awakening your goose flesh. This may be what you have been waiting for. Let's take a look at everything you may need to find out who is with you, and how you can maybe help them move on. Knowing that your loved ones are still around you may help you feel at peace, and relieve some of the anger, loneliness, and sadness you may be experiencing under the cloak of grief.

Let's take a walk through the gadget store to see what you may need to help you find out if your loved ones are around you. Knowing if your loved ones are present will make it easier to recognize any signs that you may have overlooked—this is something we will glance at in the following chapter. I would just like to add a little disclaimer here, to let you know that I am not telling you or influencing you to purchase any of the devices. Everything that will be mentioned is based on what the experts use. I do not claim to be a paranormal expert. I am a regular person who is sharing everything that I know and have researched to help people find ways to communicate with their dearly departed.

### Ghost Detectors

No, they are not labeled as such in the stores. You will ask the salesperson at the gadget store for a paranormal energy detector. These detectors have different names, but I am confident that the salesperson will help you find what you are looking for. Shopping for one of these ghost detectors or meters may be a little intimidating. You would need something that has a circuit which detects the vibrations in the magnetic field. The wrong type of detector may give false readings. You don't want to think that your loved one is around you, when in actual fact it is just a high concentration of magnetic ions floating about.

## Electromagnetic Field Meters

Another type of ghost detector gadget you could look at is the electromagnetic field meter (EMF). EMF meters are used to measure the electromagnetic radiation of the space around people. Electromagnetic radiation is recognized by identifying the energy from multiple sources such as people, electronic devices, and the earth. The detection, as recorded by the EMF, is used to calculate the electromagnetic energy from unrecognizable sources. The possibility of a presence may or may not be indicated when there is a spike in radiation levels in a certain area or space. The electromagnetic interface (EMI) is used to detect the possibility of paranormal activity. The presence of paranormal activity in the space around someone could interfere with, and potentially cause damage to, electronic devices.

## Electronic Voice Phenomena (EVP) Recorder

I have introduced you to detectors and devices. I have given you short explanations of what all these gadgets do. I have saved EVP for last because, as far as I'm concerned, this is the one that seals the deal for me. If ever you have wondered what goes on in the space around you, this is the time to sit up and take note of what may be sharing your space. I did a little extra research for this section because I believe that this is something that you can do without spending hundreds of dollars on equipment that you may only use once. You will need a voice recorder. This could be any type of digital device which you could purchase at Best Buy, or any store that sells electronics. Or, I love this, you could use your smartphone. Mobile devices have high-quality equipment, so why go out and spend unnecessary money.

The next thing you will need is a set of good quality in- or over-the-ear listening equipment such as noise-canceling headphones, earbuds, or AirPods (Wireless earphones). What you do next is ensure that the space you want to practice on is quiet and free of noises, such as the humming fridge or the snoring dog laying on your feet. When you are sure you are comfortable, you will hit record. You can ask questions, or you can have a one-sided conversation with yourself. When you feel that you are confident that you may or may not have captured something, you can stop the recording. Replay the recording and listen carefully to what, if anything, you can hear.

In the world of paranormal activity, EVP is the detection or capturing of voices on a recording device. The voices may be a mystery, or they may just be from your dearly departed loved one(s). You may even imagine that you are hearing voices because you just want to believe that your loved one is with you. Reach out to a paranormal expert, or someone that is good with technology, if you need another set of ears.

## *Paranormal Activity: Author's Thoughts*

Writing about TAPS and the *Ghost Hunters* got me thinking about a program that was on television back in 2005. The show was called *Ghost Whisperer* and featured Jennifer Love Hewitt (who played Melinda) and David Conrad (who portrayed Jim Clancy). Melinda had been born with a very special gift—the ability to see and speak to the dead. Melinda was tasked with helping the ghosts connect with their loved ones, and give them messages or ask for forgiveness. At the end of every 45-minute episode, Melinda helped the ghosts give their loved ones messages. Each message was a way to help the person be at peace with the knowledge that their loved one was moving on to the next phase of their life. They would walk away after kissing their loved ones (touching a hand, arm, or shoulder) and walk toward a light.

This is the vision I have when I think about communicating with Dad and Amadeus. Ironically, there is an episode of *Ghost Whisperer* that features a ghost dog. Melinda is the only one that can see him. She helps him cross over eventually, but it is a reminder that anything is possible. Yes, this may have been a television show, but who knows what goes on when the cameras stop rolling? See you in the next chapter.

# Chapter 8:

# Utilizing Communication Options—Contacting the Dearly Departed

- Are you ready to use the tips, tools, and tricks that you have gathered throughout this book?

- Is your mind, body, and soul ready to begin implementing the communication tools?

- Have you put fear in your backpack?

I have written this book for those of us who need to say hello or goodbye to the dearly departed. I know that I can't please everyone. I know that many people will need Botox to iron out their frowns because they don't believe in what I am saying. This book, but especially this chapter, is personal to everyone who has lost a loved one. There is no one-size-fits-all when it comes to dealing with losses and grief. Everyone has their own coping techniques. Some are content with where they are on their journey through the cloak of grief. Others are struggling to get through the days. This chapter is going to help everyone who needs reassurance that their loved ones are perhaps in that better place that everyone seems to know so much about.

I have heard so many stories about people who have been afraid to utilize the various communication options to connect them with their loved ones. Many have shared that they know that their loved ones are around, and that there is a life after this one. Many have shared that they would like to believe that there is a life after this. When asked what is holding them back, the response is that they are afraid to explore their options for fear of what others may say. I asked them what was preventing them from using a professional to help them connect with their loved ones. Most said that they didn't believe in the professionals. Others said they were afraid of who or what may join the party.

We live in a society that is surrounded by negativity. Everyone has an opinion. If your opinion does not meet the standards of others, they will begin with subtle, yet effective, manipulation techniques. Why? Are those that don't believe in a life after this hiding behind a facade? Maybe they secretly do believe that there is a life after this, but are afraid to admit it. Maybe they are afraid of what messages may come out during a consultation with a professional? I always give people the benefit of the doubt. I don't condemn people for doing something they want to do. I don't tell others how to live their lives.

## Connecting With Your Dearly Departed

You have been given many breadcrumbs since you started this book. Those breadcrumbs, when put together, should be a full loaf of bread. Your loaf of bread contains information, hints, tips, advice, stories, and just about everything you will need to learn how to communicate with your dearly departed. You have learned that you can communicate by talking, singing, praying, dancing, and even writing letters. You also learned that you can use some paranormal detection devices. But what you may want to learn more about is psychics. We mentioned psychics, but I thought it would be good to dedicate a chapter that will help you find the right person to help you. If you are reading this, then you are ready to take that next step.

Your head, heart, and mind have aligned. You know what you want to do. You have shoved all the fear, negativity, and condemnation to the back of the garden shed. You have realized that you do not need anyone's approval. You know where you stand in your faith with your deity of choice. It may have taken a couple of days, or many years, to reach the point where you want to consult with a professional. No one has to know your reasons. You are an adult, and you don't need consent. It all boils down to doing what you know you need and want to do. The decision to communicate with your loved one through a professional may be what you need to move forward with your life.

## *Who Are You Going to Call?*

The first order of business is to find a professional. This may just be the most difficult part of the whole process. I know you may be excited to find someone, but don't just decide on the first person you come across. Research the psychics you come across during your search. Find them on Google, or social media platforms. Read the reviews. I always read the one-star comments to see why people weren't happy, and then I get to the five-star reviews. I have found that most people set their expectations too high. They will accuse the psychic of being a fraud when they don't get the results that they were hoping to get.

Google will recommend many websites. Many of those websites will be third-party websites offering you this, that, and the other "if you click on this link for the low price of $4.99. Click this link now to set up your reading to avoid disappointment." Don't fall into those traps. Professional psychics will not ask you to click on any links or pay for service until you have had your consultation. Search the directories in your county to find a professional. You will notice that 90% of professional psychics have dedicated websites. You can also read testimonials from other clients.

I would like to remind you that psychics are not witches or magicians. They are regular people who have gifts that they share with everyone. They are not perfect, and they may not always give you the answers you want. They can give you hope. You may need to have more than one session before you receive what you have been yearning for. Be patient, and keep your mind open to whatever is being told to you. Make a list of questions you want to ask. Your psychic wants to help you build the bridge you want.

## Preparing For the First Visit

You may be feeling more than slightly overwhelmed. I know that there are many hints, tips, and information. I want to ensure that you are equipped with everything you may need. Some may say that I am mollycoddling. Others may say that I need to cut the apron strings and let them find their own way. It is part of my nature to give everyone the same opportunity to find everything they would need to help them. I know what it is like to be grieving. Your mind is numb. You can barely think, let alone do research. I want to cover all the bases so that you have everything you need. This chapter is your one-stop guide. You don't have to do the research. All you need is to find your inner peace, and be accepting of what your psychic has to tell you.

I would like to add here that you may experience a spark of doubt. You know that you are ready. You know what you want to do. You may have been overly excited, but then fear started creeping back into your mind. It happens to everyone. It's okay if you want to take a couple of steps back while you gather yourself. I'm not going anywhere, and this book will still be with you. Let's take a look at the "am I ready for my first psychic visit" list. You can hide behind me if you want; I'll protect you as much as I can.

### The Grief Gage

One of the most important pieces of advice I ever received was that I should not do anything in haste. The more recent the loss, the higher your expectations are when you meet with the psychic. I know—trust me—I know that you want to get there as soon as possible. Your mind is telling you that you won't get to have a clear connection the longer they are gone. Close your eyes and take a couple of slow, deep breaths. Block out any noises around you. Allow your senses to do their work. Listen, feel, and smell the space around you. I can guarantee that your loved one is with you.

### No Resistance

Be sure that this is what you want. You need to have, and maintain, an open mind. Don't enter the consultation with doubt and negativity. I have previously mentioned that you shouldn't set your level of expectation too high, but don't set it too low, either. Meet the psychic halfway. Allow them to help you with what you want. I know you are afraid, but it's not as bad as it may seem. Follow, and implement, the advice I shared in the previous paragraph.

### Peacefulness and Calmness Equates to Relaxed

Think about your loved one leading up to your first consultation. Speak to them, and tell them what your plans are. I am going to be honest with you, and tell you that you will experience stage fright when you walk into the room. Your heart will start beating faster, your breathing will become rapid, your palms will become clammy, and beads of sweat will form on your brow, the top of your lip, and in places you would rather not think about. In short, you will feel as if you are in a glass box.

Avoid the panic and follow these handy tips:

- Be confident.
- Find something in the room that you can focus on.

- Regulate your breathing by focusing on the object you chose.

- Keep your hands open.

- Relax your jaw.

- Think about your loved one.

## *Identifying That Your Loved One Is Present*

If you choose to initiate a channel of communication without the help of a psychic, you can do so by learning what signs to look for. This may be frustrating if you don't know what to look for. Your loved ones may use various ways to get your attention. You may find signs in a song you hear on the radio. You may find signs on the billboards that remind you of your loved one. You may smell something that you know is not in your home. Sometimes, the signs are so subtle that you miss them. I remember someone telling me that after their dog passed away, they heard her for three months. When asked how they knew it was their dog, they said that it was part of her nightly routine. She would walk up the short passage to the bedroom, make sure everyone was okay, and would walk back to the kitchen. They say that they still hear her, but she stuck around until she knew that a new puppy would fill the void her human felt.

Many people have these gut feelings that someone is in the room with them. I have heard people say that they have an eerie feeling that they are being watched. Others have said that they have felt something brush against them when there is no one else around. One of the most popular signs that your loved ones are trying to connect with you is through your dreams. A lot of people who dream don't make the connection between the dream and a message. They are only too happy to see the loved ones that they forget to understand what the dream was about.

Someone asked me if they could schedule visits with their dearly departed. I think it's possible, especially when you take circumstances, time of day, or moods into account. You can't see your loved ones, but they can see you. It makes sense that they will try to connect with you when you are alone or sleeping. They may try to communicate with you on a special occasion, such as a birthday or an anniversary. They may also want to let you know that they are just popping in because they could see that you needed some reassurance. It is up to each person to learn to look out for the signs that identify with their loved ones. Look out for coins in the pockets of your coats or trousers that you know weren't there before. How about the trail of feathers that are in your line of vision? The signs are all around us.

## *My 1999 Psychic Experience*

While my voice friend had disappeared, my 1999 experience did not end there. The second part of my communication-beyond-the-grave experience was one that I had never really thought I would do. I believe it would be appropriate to give Steven, my cousin, credit for the next part of my experience. Steven, who is more like a brother to me, came to me about six months after the encounter with my voice friend. He told me that he had invited a psychic to his home to do readings, and asked if I would like to be part of the experience. Truthfully, I had never had a reading done before. Curiosity is a wonderful little bug that lives in our minds. It will keep twitching and tickling your mind until you give in.

I arrived at Steven's home and walked into the living room. I didn't realize he had invited all the women in Liverpool to meet the psychic. Okay, slight exaggeration but, yes, many ladies were waiting for their chance to have their reading done by the physic. A quick glance around the room led me to believe that I was the only male waiting to meet with the psychic. I found myself a comfortable seat, and patiently waited for my turn. My turn arrived and I went through to the kitchen where the psychic was sitting at the kitchen table. I walked in, closed the kitchen door, and sat down opposite her.

## The Revelation: Part 1

The psychic started laughing the moment I sat down, and I was slightly more than shocked. Why was this lady laughing at me? Was it because I was the only male that she would be doing a reading for today? Was I the first male she had ever done a reading for? The questions were just sprouting in my mind. She assured me that she was not laughing at me; there was 'someone' in the room with us. The psychic explained that a tall gentleman was standing behind me. I listened intently as she continued to describe this gentleman. She told me that he was wearing a long coat, and a flat cap was perched on his head. Needless to say, I was very skeptical and sat there with my arms folded, not uttering a single word. The entire session lasted for approximately 45 minutes. And yes, I made notes of everything that was said. In fact, I still have the notes I made. It was an interesting experience, to say the least.

## The Revelation: Part 2

The psychic touched on my past, what is happening in the present, and what she foresaw for my future. She read her tarot cards and my palms. I believe that she also used a lot of intuition as she was guided by her spiritual guides. What she told me was stuff no one, not even Steven, would have known. The psychic spoke about Jessica, my grandma, and my life.

I knew that the psychic had missed the mark when she told me that I would be moving to the United States, where I would settle down. In the same breath, she added that Liverpool would always be my home. Once a Liverpudlian, always one. Yes, I was convinced that this lady and her guides were channeling someone else. It was 1999, and I had no intention of moving to America. Why would I move away from my family, cross the ocean and time zone, and settle in a country where I didn't know anyone? No, there was something way off with her reading… Or was there?

My life in Liverpool took on a new direction that I had never foreseen in 2001. Okay, to be fair, the psychic saw it and she informed me; but, the skeptic in me didn't take her seriously. Yes, I moved to the United States. Jessica and I moved to North Carolina where we started a new life in a country far from our beginnings. We set down our roots and, 20 years later, we are still happily living in a country that adopted us. Liverpool is still my home. My Mum, sister, brother-in-law, niece, nephew, uncles, aunts, and cousins are all there. I heard someone say something which I have adapted to fit me: "You can take the man out of Liverpool, but you can't take Liverpool out of the man." How did the psychic know that this would happen? How did she know that I would move, as she had predicted?

### The Revelation: Part 3

The skeptic in me wanted to ask the psychic one question. This question had been brewing since the start of the reading. I figured that it was safe to ask my question after the reading had ended. "Who was the tall man that you mentioned was standing behind me?" I asked, looking her straight in the eyes. (I was trying to see if she was lying, or about to lie to me.)

She smiled at me, not looking away, and said: "It was your grandfather." Wait a minute, Dad's dad was visiting me? She went to describe him as she had seen him. He was a man's man. He commanded respect wherever he went. He would walk into a room and, if there were no open seats, someone would offer up their seat to him. He went to work every day. He would stop at the local pub for a pint of beer with the other men. He would drink his pint of beer and head home for dinner. The psychic mentioned that he was a very strict man, which he now regretted. She also mentioned that he had worked in the United States for several months. I had never heard about that, because my grandpa had passed away when I was five years old.

Lightbulbs and fireworks started going off in my head. I told the psychic about the evil voice I had heard in my house. I asked her if she would be able to tell me who it could have been. She smiled again and declared that it was him—it was my grandpa! This revelation led me to ask one more question: "Why the scary voice?" The response was that he wanted to get my attention. My grandpa believed that my life was going nowhere. He believed that I could do so much more. He wanted me to wake up and shake up. The psychic said that my grandpa wasn't here to harm or scare me, but he did want to protect me.

I thanked the psychic for her insights into my life. I handed the payment for the reading over to her. She looked at me again, one of those intense stares, and informed me that I have a gift as well. I didn't know what she meant, and my blank stare led her to elaborate: "You can communicate with spirits and the dearly departed."

## The Revelation: Part 4

I went straight to my parent's house when I left Steven. I had some questions that needed answers. I made myself a cup of tea, and sat down with Mum and Dad. I was honest with them and told them that I had been to see a psychic. I told them everything that she had told me during her reading, as well as the information about my grandpa. I remember looking at Dad and seeing that he was shocked. He left the living room without a word. I was worried that he was angry because of what I had done. I shouldn't have worried because he returned with a black and white photograph of my grandpa. The photograph shows him sitting on the Woolworths building in New York City!

More lightbulbs and fireworks going off in my mind. At this point, I am slightly more than stunned at everything I had learned, and continue to learn. How did the psychic know that my grandpa had worked in the United States? I didn't even know that. I proceeded to tell Dad everything that the psychic had shared about my grandpa's personality. Dad nodded in agreement and reaffirmed that my grandpa was exactly as the psychic had described him.

# Chapter 9:

# Preparing for the Final

# Descent—Wrapping It Up

I started on this journey because I had an insatiable hunger for knowledge. I wanted, and needed, to know what happens when we die. As much as I want to communicate with Dad and other family members, I want to be prepared for the day that I cross the threshold between the two worlds. I would love to know if I will also be sitting on the heavenly perch, and keeping a close eye on Jessica as I know Dad is doing with me. I want to make sure that she treats others with the same respect that I have instilled into her since she was little. I doubt I will cuff her on the ear if she steps out of line, but I may do something annoying that will let her know that I am watching. I have often heard people saying that they will come back and haunt their loved ones if they did anything against their wishes. I recently heard a mom tell her teen that they would be the death of her, to which the teen replied: "Oh great, so I can look forward to you being annoyed from wherever you're going." I have found that people enjoy making jokes about the afterlife. I have also seen the look in their eyes as they say it, which leads me to believe that they hope that their jokes will become a reality.

# Journey of Discovery

I wanted to use this chapter to revisit some previous topics that have been touched on and discussed. I wanted to include a couple of stories, and fill you with the hope that you have been yearning for. You know what you are looking for, and if I have learned anything it is that when you want something, no one can change your mind. I could have mentioned that when we started on this discovery journey, but you needed to know and understand that you have choices. I wasn't going to dictate what you should be doing, nor was I going to tell you that what you are doing is wrong. I am just a regular guy who goes to work, does gardening, goes on bike rides, and dabbles in writing non-fiction self-help books. You can do anything you want, because you are in charge of your destiny.

The journey of discovery has not been as easy as one may think. Writing this book has opened a couple of scabs that had healed (or so I thought). I was remembering things that I had locked away under a thick pile of dust in the archives. I have found healing and comfort in researching, writing, and sharing personal stories from my life and those of others. I asked multiple people why they were sharing their stories with me, and not writing their own books. The majority of those I spoke to told me that their stories needed a different voice that had a greater viewing audience. I am grateful to everyone who has shared, and continue to share, their stories with me.

## Retracing the Steps

I have shared the definitions and meanings about life and death from reputable sources. I have given you science- and religious-backed facts and findings from scientists and researchers. I took you on a tour to visit various religions. You learned what a couple of the religious Christian denominations believed about death and the afterlife. A jump back in time took you to a couple of the ancient civilizations and non-denominational religions. You left the ancient civilizations armed with a truckload of knowledge.

There was no time to slow down and smell the roses. The hunger for knowledge is the driving force behind your curiosity. You were introduced to the heroes in their professions, the ones that guide us in and out of this world, and to those who help our bodies to return to the earth. I introduced you to the world of paranormal detection experts. You were introduced to a couple of the essential detection devices that you may need to do some investigation around your home. Being the nice person that I am, I snuck in a little "do it yourself" tutorial.

I allowed the naysayers to join us on this journey. I have nothing to hide. I am pretty certain that they were looking for any hints that I was trying to control how people think. I may have shared a couple of times that this journey through time and space required everyone to have an open mind. I concluded that nobody has to defend themselves against those who don't allow others to be who they want to be. You will not find any type of bullying in this book. Everyone—no matter where they come from or what their religion, gender, or ethnicity is—everyone is allowed to claim a piece of the sun, sky, and ground they walk on.

## A Slight Detour

I have dedicated a chapter to exploring the science associated with near-death experiences. The goal, and hope, of this book was to give you some evidence that your dearly departed was waiting for you on the other side of the threshold, between the two worlds. I believe that I gave you as much information as I could find. There were stories from those who witnessed the smiles, the tears, and the fears as their loved ones left the physical world. Those that stayed behind witnessed *something* they couldn't put their finger on. It was that *something* that brought you here. You came here looking for answers. You embarked on this journey with trepidation, unsure of what you would learn. You may even have been told that you are putting your religion in jeopardy. Some may have said that you are wasting your time and money. But, I know that deep down in your heart, you believe everything that I am saying.

This journey of discovery has been personally handcrafted to fill the requirements of each individual. I am your guide and the voice that tells you it is okay to have hope, and it is okay to believe that your dearly departed are waiting for you. You may have tried all the communication methods that have been mentioned in this book, and nothing seemed to work for you. Don't give up hope, and don't stop believing. Try again on another day, at another time, or in another location. Remember that you have to build that line of communication by having an open mind. What may come naturally to someone may require a little more work from others. I wish I could tell you that communicating with our dearly departed is as easy as punching in a couple of numbers, or sending text messages.

Practice patience when you start using all the tools you have been given. I know that I have been lurking around every other corner, and popping up between the words, to remind you that you need to have an open mind. I am going to put an emphasis right here, as a final reminder, to practice being patient. I know, and I understand, that we live in a fast-paced world. You only have to close your eyes, and you feel the earth moving. I bet you didn't know that you are in control of your world. You don't have to conform to the ways of the world. You may hit the pause button whenever you want. The world will not slow down for everyone else, but it will for you.

Don't give up trying to communicate with your dearly departed. Look out for any signs that may have been left for you. Don't dismiss what you may label as being obvious. I'll tell you a little secret, but don't tell anyone else: those obvious signs may be the recognition you have been waiting for.

## *Life After This: The Amadeus Story*

Writing this book, as I have mentioned, has re-opened a couple of wounds that I thought had started healing. It is no secret that I miss Dad. It is no secret that I miss Amadeus, my dog. Amadeus crossed over the rainbow bridge during the writing and editing phase of my last book. He was nearly 15-years old, which is a pretty good age for a member of the four-legged family. Amadeus was my best friend. I would even put my *crazy* out here to inform you that he was a human living in the body of a dog. I have honestly never known any other dog like him.

Amadeus had a heart murmur. He reached a point in his old life where he couldn't run without collapsing. His energy and oxygen levels were not where they once were. He wasn't suffering, he wasn't in pain, and he was eating and drinking. When humans reach a certain age, the body becomes a little temperamental, and one is reminded to slow down. This is where we were with Amadeus. He wanted to keep going, but his body and his organs tried to tell him to slow down.

Amadeus' health started declining in November 2021. He started coughing and gagging. I took him to the vet, who informed me that Amadeus had fluid surrounding his lungs. The fluid was suffocating him, and putting even more strain on his lungs. The doctor kept him overnight, and my dad-dog heart could barely hold it together because his son was not with him. The doctor informed me that he had given Amadeus oxygen throughout the night. He sent us home with a warning that it was only a temporary fix. Two days later, I had to take Amadeus back to the vet. I called the following morning to find out how he was, and they told me that he was okay, but that I needed to make some very difficult choices.

I picked him up again and brought him home. I didn't want to think about the end. Amadeus walked around the backyard, as if to make sure everything was as it was. He marked his territory, as always, on all his favorite bushes. I watched him, sadness filling me because he was oblivious that it was going to be his last day with me. Jessica drove three hours to come and say goodbye to him. We took him back to the vet later that afternoon. We held him in our arms as the doctor administered the shot. We told Amadeus how much we loved him. We told him that he needed to go and find Dad, and that he would show him around. Amadeus left the physical world in our arms, surrounded by his loved ones.

I can't put into words the pain I felt, and still do. Amadeus has been with us every single day since his passing. Alison and I have his ashes in special rings. It was devastating losing Dad. I was there when he took his last breath. But seeing Amadeus, my dog, my son, and my best friend take his last breath was different than my experience with losing Dad. It is hard to explain, and I wouldn't know where or how to begin. I will admit that I am overcome with guilt when I cry for Amadeus and not for Dad. I miss them both, but missing Amadeus is a different kind of longing. Amadeus and I had a nightly routine for so many years. That routine was broken in the blink of an eye. It was my responsibility to take him out for his last toilet run. I still go outside every evening before I go to bed; the only difference is that Amadeus isn't with me—or is he? Maybe Amadeus is letting me know that he is still with me. He may even be marking his favorite bushes when I go out every night. I do believe that Dad is sharing his heavenly perch with Amadeus. Together they are watching over us, and ensuring that we are being good people.

# Conclusion

I decided to put my heart and grief into words when I wrote *Keep Calm and Cope With Grief.* I chose to share my experience with others because I felt a void when Dad passed away. I had come to despise hearing the obligatory: "I know how you feel" and "he is in a better place." Firstly, no one experiences a loss the same way. Each person feels and deals with the loss of a loved one in different ways. Secondly, the best place for Dad is at home, in Liverpool, with Mum. I was already tangled between the dark layers of the cloak of grief, when I suffered yet another loss. Not many people understood how I was feeling, or what I was experiencing.

I wrote this book because I wanted answers to the questions I asked in the Introduction. I have experienced so many changes in the last three years of my life. I knew that I may not get all the answers that I needed, and I was fine with that. I know that I have done the best I could do to give myself, and my readers, as much information as possible. I know that many people will not agree with what has been written. Everyone's point of view is different. I'm not a bully, nor have I ever been one, and I'm not about to start now because I'm writing books. Remember, I have Dad and Amadeus sitting on their heavenly perch. I love my ears, and I love my ankles. Dad will reach down and cuff me on the ear, and Amadeus will bite my ankles if I were to intentionally hurt someone.

I believe that I have given you everything that you will need to answer all the questions that have been asked since you embarked on this journey with me. I know, without a doubt, that our loved ones are trying to communicate with us. I believe my physical body is on loan to me. I know that my soul and spirit will return to my Maker, where I will be reunited with everyone who is, and was, near and dear to me. Don't be afraid to reach out to your loved ones. Speak to them, because they will hear you. Write them letters, because they will read them. Have dance parties, because they will be dancing with you.

# Reflection

I wrote the following section during the research phase of this book. I have included it in the Conclusion because I believe that it will help those that may still be skeptical. This may just be the little nudge you needed.

"While sitting here, doing my research for this book, I sat back and thought about Dad. I closed my eyes, and wondered if he was here with me. I needed a break. I needed a distraction from focusing on all the information I was soaking up. What does a guy do when he needs a break? He goes car shopping online. I'm always looking for trucks. I opened a new tab on the browser and searched for local car dealerships. I opened the website I wanted, and clicked on the first truck that came up. There were 22 pictures associated with this particular truck. I clicked through all the photos, and came to a dead stop at picture number 14. My hand was frozen, and I stared at the photo. The image was of a dashboard and media screen in the center console. The display on the media screen is what grabbed my attention. That particular image showed the time of the day, which was 11 a.m., the outside temperature of 80°F, the radio station that was playing, 96.1, and the song that was playing was "I Am Alive" by the Parlotones.

I kid you not. I was wondering if Dad was with me, and then I see an image that displays "I Am Alive," and my jaw drops. Now, I believe in coincidences, but at that moment in time, just after I had asked a question, I clicked on that truck and saw that image? I could have clicked on any of the hundreds of vehicles or thousands of photos, but I clicked on that truck, that photo, at that time, and it showed a media screen with "I Am Alive" displayed. I believe that it was Dad answering me. He was letting me know that *he is alive*, that *he is okay*, and that *he is around me*."

## *The End of the Journey*

We have reached the end of our discovery journey. I am leaving you with a lot of information to help you find your way through the cloak of grief. Always do what is right for you. Don't be afraid to be curious. Don't be afraid to have hope. Don't ever be afraid to dream.

May I be so forward as to ask if you would leave a review of what you thought of this book? Please share your experience with communication with your dearly departed in the review section. I would love for other readers to see that they have nothing to fear. Sharing your story, and your review, will help many people feel that they have an army surrounding them. Be blessed, and may your God go with you.

# References

Acker, L. (2018, October 23). *10 ways to communicate with the dead, according to an expert.* Oregonlive. https://www.oregonlive.com/life-and-culture/erry-2018/10/681847055948/10-ways-to-communicate-with-th.html

Allard, S. (2020, September 3). *5 Things to know about Hindus and death.* Hindu American Foundation. https://www.hinduamerican.org/blog/5-things-to-know-about-hindus-and-death

The Atlantic Paranormal Society. (2022, March 12). In *Wikipedia.* https://en.wikipedia.org/wiki/The_Atlantic_Paranormal_Society

Ayoub, O. (2021, July 31). *Life after death in Islam: The concept and the 14 stages of afterlife.* Zamzam Blogs. https://zamzam.com/blog/life-after-death-in-islam/

Banks, P. (2020, November 8). *How to prepare yourself for the first meeting with a psychic.* Wingman. https://get-a-wingman.com/how-to-prepare-yourself-for-the-first-meeting-with-a-psychic/

Bible Study Tools. (n.d.). Life. In *Biblestudytools.com dictionary.* https://www.biblestudytools.com/dictionary/life/

Books, S. (2016, September 21). *15 Afterlife beliefs from different religions.* TheRichest.

https://www.therichest.com/most-shocking/15-afterlife-beliefs-from-different-religions

*Ceremonies and religious roles.* (n.d.). Ancient Aztecs. https://aztecjourneybyjenna.weebly.com/ceremonies-and-religous-roles.html

The Church of Jesus Christ of Latter-Day Saints. (n.d.). *There is life after death | ComeUntoChrist.*https://www.churchofjesuschrist.org/comeuntochrist/africasouth/beliefs/life-after-death

Dockray, H. (2013, May 20). *Ancient Aztec perspective on death and afterlife.* Christi Center. https://christicenter.org/2013/02/ancient-aztec-perspective-on-death-and-afterlife/

Elliott, P. M. (2011, January 5). *What is the biblical definition of death?* Teaching the Word Ministries. http://www.teachingtheword.org/apps/articles/?articleid=74731&columnid=5435

Freund, A. (2019, April 17). *The science of dying.* DW. https://www.dw.com/en/the-science-of-dying/a-48372592

FRONTLINE PBS. (2015, February 13). *How doctors tell patients they're dying | Being mortal* [Video]. YouTube. https://www.youtube.com/watch?v=jaB9M8B_Tuw

Holden, J. M., Greyson, B., & James, D. (2009). *The handbook of near-death experiences : Thirty years of investigation.* Praeger Publishers.

Janssen, S. (2021, October). *Near death experiences: Will our dogs be waiting for us?* The Bark.

https://thebark.com/content/near-death-experiences-will-our-dogs-be-waiting-us

Kelly Clarkson Show. (2019, October 9). *"Long Island Medium" Theresa Caputo gives Kelly Clarkson & her stylist an emotional psychic reading* [Video]. YouTube. https://www.youtube.com/watch?v=BLjba5vTLCI

Kessler, S. (2022, April 25). *What does the catholic church teach about the afterlife?* Cake. https://www.joincake.com/blog/catholic-afterlife/

Khan Academy. (n.d.). *What is life? (article) | Intro to biology.* https://www.khanacademy.org/science/biology/intro-to-biology/what-is-biology/a/what-is-life

*Learn more about Jehovah's Witness and cremation.* (2016, January 14). Neptune Society. https://www.neptunesociety.com/cremation-information-articles/jehovahs-witness-and-cremation

Long, J. (2014). Near-Death Experiences Evidence for Their Reality. *Missouri Medicine, 111*(5), 372. https://www.ncbi.nlm.nih.gov/pmc/articles/PMC6172100/

MacDonald, F. (2015, April 27). *There are seven types of near-death experiences, according to research.* ScienceAlert. https://www.sciencealert.com/there-are-seven-types-of-near-death-experiences-according-to-new-research

*Maintaining a connection with the dead in ancient Egypt.* (2021, November 18). Australian Museum. https://australian.museum/learn/cultures/international-collection/ancient-egyptian/mantaining-a-connection-with-the-dead-in-ancient-egypt/

Marsh, M. (2016, March 28). The Near-Death Experience: A Reality Check? *Humanities, 5*(2), 18. https://doi.org/10.3390/h5020018

Meder, A. L. (2022, March 9). *How to communicate with a deceased loved one.* Amanda Linette Meder. https://www.amandalinettemeder.com/blog/2014/11/5/6-things-you-didnt-know-about-connecting-with-a-deceased-loved-one

Merriam-Webster. (n.d.-a). Apocalypse. In *Merriam-Webster.com dictionary.* Retrieved May 24, 2022, from https://www.merriam-webster.com/dictionary/apocalypse

Merriam-Webster. (n.d.-b). *Death.* In *Merriam-Webster.com dictionary.* Retrieved May 24, 2022, from https://www.merriam-webster.com/dictionary/death

Merriam-Webster. (n.d.-c). Déjà vu. In *Merriam-Webster.com dictionary.* Retrieved May 24, 2022, from https://www.merriam-webster.com/dictionary/d%C3%A9j%C3%A0%20vu

Merriam-Webster. (n.d.-d). Life. In *Merriam-Webster.com dictionary.* Retrieved May 24, 2022, from https://www.merriam-webster.com/dictionary/life

Merriam-Webster. (n.d.-e). Near-Death experience. In *Merriam-Webster.com dictionary.* Retrieved May 24, 2022, from https://www.merriam-webster.com/dictionary/near-death%20experience

Merriam-Webster. (n.d.-f). Soul. In *Merriam-Webster.com dictionary.* Retrieved May 24, 2022, from https://www.merriam-webster.com/dictionary/soul

Merriam-Webster. (n.d.-g). Spirit. In *Merriam-Webster.com dictionary*. Retrieved May 24, 2022, from https://www.merriam-webster.com/dictionary/spirit

Moshakis, A. (2021, March 7). *What do near-death experiences mean, and why do they fascinate us?* The Guardian. https://www.theguardian.com/society/2021/mar/07/the-space-between-life-and-death

Motamed, A. (2019, January 31). *Ancient Egyptian afterlife beliefs*. Trips in Egypt. https://www.tripsinegypt.com/ancient-egyptian-afterlife-beliefs/

*New International Version*. (1993). BibleGateway.com. https://www.biblegateway.com

The Occult Museum. (2017, September 8). *10 Funeral home workers share their most macabre and morbid stories*.http://www.theoccultmuseum.com/10-funeral-home-workers-share-their-most-macabre-and-morbid-stories/

Oliveto, J. (2020, July 2). *5 Aztec death views & rituals explained*. Cake. https://www.joincake.com/blog/how-do-aztecs-view-death/

Parnia, S., Spearpoint, K., de Vos, G., Fenwick, P., Goldberg, D., Yang, J., Zhu, J., Baker, K., Killingback, H., McLean, P., Wood, M., Zafari, A. M., Dickert, N., Beisteiner, R., Sterz, F., Berger, M., Warlow, C., Bullock, S., Lovett, S., & McPara, R. M. S. (2014, October 6). AWARE—AWAreness during REsuscitation—A prospective study. *Resuscitation, 85*(12), 1799–1805. https://doi.org/10.1016/j.resuscitation.2014.09.004

Pascagliatti, J. (2017, May 17). *15 Strangest things doctors heard people say before dying.* TheRichest. https://www.therichest.com/shocking/15-strangest-things-doctors-heard-people-say-before-dying/

Pavlina, E. (2011, November 17). *How can I get a deceased loved one to communicate with me?* Erin Pavlina. https://www.erinpavlina.com/blog/2011/11/how-can-i-get-a-deceased-loved-one-to-communicate-with-me/

Rathore, A. (2020, April 10). *The electronics of paranormal manifestations.* Electronics for You. https://www.electronicsforu.com/technology-trends/tech-focus/the-electronics-of-paranormal-manifestations

Sagan, D., Sagan, C., & Margulis, L. (2022, January 27). Life. In *Encyclopædia Britannica.* https://www.britannica.com/science/life

Smith, C. (2019, December 3). *7 Things to do before you visit a psychic medium.* TheLeafsNation. https://theleafsnation.com/2019/12/02/7-things-to-do-before-you-visit-a-psychic-medium/

Strong, A. (2019, November 17). *Can I contact a deceased loved one? 4 Ways to connect!* Intuitive Development & Guidance by Ashley Strong. https://lightloveandspirit.com/contact-deceased-loved-one/

Tetrault, S. (2022, May 3). *What did ancient Egyptians believe about the life after death?* Cake. https://www.joincake.com/blog/egyptian-afterlife/

Wagner, S. (2019, January 16). *15 Steps to recording ghost voices with EVP in 15 steps.* LiveAbout. https://www.liveabout.com/how-to-record-evp-2594034

White, L. (2017, March 17). *What really happens after you die.* Beliefnet. https://www.beliefnet.com/inspiration/articles/what-really-happens-after-you-die.aspx

WikiHow. (2021, November 16). *How to talk to the dead.* https://www.wikihow.com/Talk-to-the-Dead

# Image References

Allen, John. (n.d). *Grandad on the Woolworth building* [Image]. John Allen.

Almasi, H. (2020, October 15). *A Father and his daughter praying in a mosque in Yazd, Iran* [Image]. Unsplash. https://unsplash.com/photos/kPWfbe65lb4

Bezanger, J. (2021, August 3). *Temple of Edfu, Egypt* [Image]. Unsplash. https://unsplash.com/photos/DfTFJHHOiB4

Boca, C. (2017, September 20). *Afternoon tea break* [Image]. Unsplash. https://unsplash.com/photos/rz6sgZkA9Vc

Eberly, T. (2021, November 27). *Person holding book page with string lights* [Image]. Unsplash. https://unsplash.com/photos/wnrxQGBhbh8

Grandahl, L. (2018, January 11). *You never know what you'll find in New York* [Image]. Unsplash. https://unsplash.com/photos/zf7rb2MF3ok

Hendry, P. (2017, March 13). [*Person with dog sitting on Grand Canyon cliff*] [Image]. Unsplash. https://unsplash.com/photos/jd0hS7Vhn_A

Korpa, J. (2018, July 3). *Long exposure couple* [Image]. Unsplash. https://unsplash.com/photos/tzQkuviIuHU

Lambeck, A. (2019, July 30). *Butterfly@Mariposario in Benalmadena* [Image]. Unsplash. https://unsplash.com/photos/5VC4thmwMms

Lázaro, J. (2017, December 14). [*Black and white digital heart beat monitor at 97 display*] [Image]. Unsplash. https://unsplash.com/photos/0lrJo37r6Nk

Lee, D. (2021, September 25). *HD photo by Derek Lee* [Image]. Unsplash. https://unsplash.com/photos/-AikVQg0P4s

McCutcheon, S. (2019, July 2). Experimental edit. *To me this feels like soulmates touching after death* [Image]. Unsplash. https://unsplash.com/photos/r6_xcsNg0kw

McFadden, M. (2018, June 26). [*Lighted votive candle lot*] [Image]. Unsplash. https://unsplash.com/photos/BWVQ7ANNB5s

Meyers, D. (2019, July 21). [*White Clouds*] [Image]. Unsplash. https://unsplash.com/photos/f1WMJR8pLqo

Michel E. (2021, September 6). *First aid workers practicing CPR* [Image]. Unsplash. https://unsplash.com/photos/fSO8pdTu8Pk

National Cancer Institute. (2020, January 22). *Cancer Surgeons* [Image]. Unsplash. https://unsplash.com/photos/701-FJcjLAQ

Nickson, R. (2019, May 28). *[Group of people sitting on rocks overlooking mountain]* [Image]. Unsplash. https://unsplash.com/photos/smJ6XsYy8gA

Nohassi, M. (2017, March 28). *Without wings I can feel free* [Image]. Unsplash. https://unsplash.com/photos/odxB5oIG_iA

Voice + Video. (2020, March 26). *Black and silver camera film* [Image]. Unsplash. https://unsplash.com/photos/ytfy-6cEBjM

Wyron A. (2018, February 16). *Psychic vision made in LA* [Image]. Unsplash. https://unsplash.com/photos/GY38n9WKjQI

Printed in Great Britain
by Amazon

42353503R00081